LEADERSHIP SECRETS OF AMERICA'S FIRST LADIES

Jacqueline Berger

"The First Ladies Lady™"

Published by Roserita Books

Books are available at special discounts when purchased in bulk for premiums and sales promotions, as well as for fundraising or educational uses. Special editions or book excerpts can be created to customer specifications. For details and further information contact:

Special Sales Director
"The First Ladies Lady™"
1534 N. Moorpark Rd., #228
Thousand Oaks, CA 91360-5129
Phone: (805) 497-8994
Email: firstladies.lady@verizon.net

For information or to book events contact
the Special Sales Director, above.
www.firstladieslady.com

Cataloging-in-Publication Data:

ISBN-13   978-0-9817041-3-5
ISBN-10   0-9817041-3-1

Cover design and interior layout by Teagarden Designs

Printed in the United States of America

First Printing: 2016

10 9 8 7 6 5 4 3 2 1

WHAT PEOPLE ARE SAYING ABOUT LEADERSHIP SECRETS OF AMERICA'S FIRST LADIES

"Jacqueline is an amazing speaker, author and business leader. If you're ready to become a better leader and achieve more success and happiness, then read and absorb the strategies in this brilliant book by my friend Jacqueline Berger!"

James Malinchak
Featured on ABCs Hit TV Show, *Secret Millionaire*
Author of the Top-Selling Book, *Millionaire Success Secrets*
Founder, www.MillionaireFreeBook.com

"Jacqueline Berger combined her personal knowledge of corporate leadership, with her personal experience as a business owner to deliver a sensible step by step guide for improving your life and career opportunities!"

Jill Lublin
Three Time Best-Selling Author,
International Speaker, Top PR Guru
www.publicitycrashcourse.com

"Lesson learned. Ms. Berger has shown how anyone can turn *anything* into an opportunity and turn that opportunity into unprecedented success."

Kevin Harrington
Original Shark on the Hit TV Show *Shark Tank* &
Inventor of the Infomercial

"Jacqueline's knowledge of history brings inspiration to future leaders and innovative concepts to experienced leaders, assisting both to move forward in their careers."

Joe Theismann
NFL World Champion & Entrepreneur

"This wonderful, inspiring book shows individuals how to realize their full potential for greater influence and leadership in life."

Brian Tracy
Author of *How the Best Leaders Lead*
President Brian Tracy International

"Ms. Berger and the esteemed company she references have given these tried and true Leadership strategies a fresh spin. A great read and valuable handbook for success."

Craig Duswalt
Speaker, Author, Radio Host and Creator of Craig Duswalt
Marketing Programs, Former Manager of Axl Rose of the
Rock-n-Roll Band Guns N' Roses

"Jacqueline Berger has done a great job of capturing the true grit of America's First Ladies and showing us how they have modeled *being of service* as the mark of a true leader. I felt stirred by a renewed motivation, remembering that each of us, regardless of our platform, can make a difference."

Sudip Bose, MD, FACEP, FAAEM
Featured physician on hit worldwide reality TV show "Untold Stories of the ER," Iraq war veteran, recognized as a "CNN Hero" for receiving the Bronze Star and servicing as the U.S. physician who treated Saddam Hussein after his capture, Recognized as one of the "Leading Physicians of the World" by the IAHCP (International Association of Healthcare Professionals), Founder of a non-profit charity, www.TheBattleContinues.org

"*Leadership Secrets of America's First Ladies* is a well-wrought, well-researched and well-considered work of great originality and clearly much effort. Jacqueline Berger has taken biographical facts of First Ladies and animated them with a timeless relevancy. She has woven a tapestry with new colors, threading through it the most important lessons to be learned from their external struggles and internal conflicts, not only giving us these familiar historical figures with an illuminated humanity but examples of leadership that every person, of every age, gender and background can draw upon. *Leadership Secrets of America's First Ladies* draws out the subtext of these individuals, showing them to be as human as us all."

Carl Sferrazza Anthony
Author, Historian, Screenwriter and Journalist
National First Ladies' Library Historian
www.firstladies.org

"Jacqueline Berger is the true First Ladies lady. Her passion for the subject matter and respect for these ladies shines through at the turn of every page. I have sat and talked with Jacqueline for hours, and I have read all of her books. I hang on every word she speaks and every sentence she writes. When we part ways, I am always looking forward to the next conversation or book."

Andrew Och
Award Winning TV producer who documented the lives of every "First Lady of the United States." The "C-SPAN" series, "First Ladies: Influence and Image" The First Ladies Man www.firstladiesman.com

"This is a wonderful book! Jacqueline Berger has written a delightful and insightful guide to leadership as seen through the lives of America's First Ladies. Most books on leadership follow the great men of history, ignoring the fact that they were partnered by incredibly talented, strong, resourceful women. A must read for all women in business everywhere!"

Chellie Campbell
Author of *The Wealthy Spirit* and
From Worry to Wealthy

MOTIVATE AND INSPIRE OTHERS!

"Share This Book"

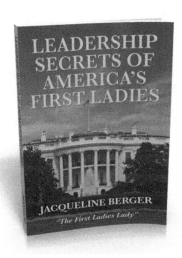

Retail $24.95

Special Quantity Discounts

5-20 Books	$21.95
21-99 Books	$18.95
100-499 Books	$15.95
500-999 Books	$10.95
1,000+ Books	$8.95

To Place an Order Contact:

"The First Ladies Lady™"
1534 N. Moorpark Rd., #228
Thousand Oaks, CA 91360-5129
Phone: (805) 497-8994
Email: firstladies.lady@verizon.net

Dedicated to my grandchildren
The next generation of leaders...

Rachel, Jeremy, Jake, Ryan and Sarah

CONTENTS

Acknowledgements 11

Introduction 13

Leaders Have A Positive Attitude 15
    —Martha Washington

Leaders are Visionaries 21
    —Abigail Adams

Leaders Build Good Relationships 27
    —Dolley Madison

Leaders Are Confident 31
    — Louisa Adams

Leaders Share The Glory 37
    —Sarah Polk

Leaders have Integrity 41
    —Lucy Hayes

Leaders View Failure as Opportunity 45
    —Frances Cleveland

Leaders are Persuaders 51
    —Caroline Harrison

Leaders are Principled 55
    —Edith Roosevelt

Leaders Plan 5-10 Years Ahead 59
    —Helen Taft

Leaders Focus on the Mission 65
    —Edith Wilson

Leaders Control Their Destiny 69
    —Florence Harding

Leaders are Undaunted 73
 —*Lou Hoover*

Leaders Grow More Leaders 77
 —*Eleanor Roosevelt*

Leaders Lead Without Titles 83
 —*Mamie Eisenhower*

Leaders Strive for Excellence 87
 —*Jacqueline Kennedy*

Leaders are Responsible 91
 —*Lady Bird Johnson*

Leaders are Willing to Serve 95
 —*Pat Nixon*

Leaders Communicate Effectively 99
 —*Betty Ford*

Leaders are Advocates 103
 —*Rosalynn Carter*

Leaders Are Readers Of People 107
 —*Nancy Reagan*

Leaders have a Sense of Humor 113
 —*Barbara Bush*

Leaders Take Calculated Risks 119
 —*Hillary Clinton*

Leaders are Positive Role Models 123
 — *Laura Bush*

Leaders are Innovators 127
 —*Michelle Obama*

About the Author 131

Acknowledgements

THOUGH MANY HOURS of solitary writing went into this book, I am acutely aware that I was never alone in the process. If not for the support, effort and encouragement of family, friends and professionals, *Leadership Secrets of America's First Ladies* would not be a reality. My heartfelt appreciation goes to each and every one.

Always first and foremost, my deepest appreciation to my husband Bruce for his endless loving support and understanding. Unlike the naiveté we shared during the writing of my first books, he understood all too well what this project entailed and the necessary sacrifices he would have to make. And still, he supported unconditionally the decision to move forward.

To my colleague and friend, Barbara Renee, for her commentary and inspired recommendations throughout this process. She spent countless hours of fact-finding and research, saving me weeks of work.

To Ann Rea, my friend, associate and mentor, words alone are insufficient thanks for her superb editing, insightful wisdom and overall astuteness. The timing of her availability truly rescued this endeavor.

If not for the vision and persistent belief of my business coach, James Malinchak, ***Leadership Secrets of America's First Ladies*** would never have been written. Due to my friend Pam Garvin's intellectual acuity, one very important First Lady leader may have gone unacknowledged. And to my sister Lynda Hendon, who always said "yes" to reading another paragraph or answering "just one more" grammar question.

Finally, but certainly not least, my sincere thanks to my immediate family and inner circle of friends, beginning with Shari Brody, all of whom never wavered in their support, encouragement and praise. I am truly blessed and most grateful to have such individuals in my life!

INTRODUCTION

LEADERSHIP AS A concept can be traced back to the Greek philosopher, Plato. Various theories have been discussed for decades; however, it was not until 1979 that the first doctoral program in Leadership Studies was established at the University of San Diego. Today it continues to be one of the fastest growing academic fields in higher education.

Although some people may come to it more instinctively, anyone can successfully learn, develop and implement proven leadership skills. Aware of it or not—like it or not—our actions demonstrate leadership or lack thereof on a daily basis. Reflection on the suggestions and questions included at the end of each chapter in this book will help you move forward. Take the time to write down your responses and then take action!

As a corporate executive, businesswoman and historian, having studied America's First Ladies for over four decades, I hold them in the highest esteem. With grace and decorum, they accepted the relentless invasion into their private lives, along with the many challenges that come with the most *difficult, unpaid* and often *unappreciated* job imaginable!

For many of the women highlighted in this book, common sense, intuition and will were their rules of engagement. For others, education and study guided their thinking and actions. All of them have stood as pillars of strength, while at the side of and learning from the nation's Chief Executive.

To be a leader, you need not have a title or the desire to guide a country. Be it in your home, workplace, community or the board room, the skills and qualities discussed in this book will improve your life, as well as the lives of those you might or hope to influence.

The invaluable life lessons and leadership skills I learned from my lifelong study of America's First Ladies assisted me in my corporate experience, and I continue to find them relevant, effective and inspiring.

1

LEADERS HAVE A POSITIVE ATTITUDE

"I am still determined to be cheerful and to be happy, in whatever situation I may be; for I have also learned from experience that the greater part of our happiness or misery depends on our dispositions and not our circumstances."

—*Martha Washington*

IT IS UNDENIABLE that our attitude makes a difference. Attitude determines our feelings, our thinking, our behavior, and even our outcomes. For better or worse, attitude is contagious and better yet, it is a learned tendency. The worse part is that a bad attitude is like a virus and quickly spreads.

Henry Ford, founder of the Ford Motor Company, was famously quoted, "Whether you say you can or you can't; you're right either way." Lou Holtz, legendary college football coach and former analyst for ESPN put it this way, "Life is ten percent what happens to you and ninety percent how you respond to it." I would go so far as to say, attitude makes your leadership and it is the most valuable asset a person can have.

Leaders recognize that their energy and attitude heavily impacts the mood and environment of their team. A positive attitude effects quality, productivity, service and alliance with clients and customers, all of which profoundly impacts the success of their organization. Furthermore, it inspires people to be the best they can be and achieve as much as they can—which is also a leader's role.

An excellent example of a positive leadership attitude, is Martha Washington. Born in the eighteenth century, the lead quote of this chapter demonstrates that Martha understood that her happiness did not depend on her circumstances. A positive attitude proved crucial throughout her arduous life.

Widowed at just twenty-six, after already having lost two children, Martha was determined to keep her large plantation working and viable. With two other children to support and only a negligible education, a pessimistic or defeatist attitude could have proven disastrous for her. Instead she chose to deal with her sorrow and what could have been overwhelming circumstances, productively. Martha asked a lot of questions and sought advice from others more experienced. She learned the necessities and proved herself to be hard working with sound values.

With the American Revolution on the horizon, life after marriage to George Washington did not get much easier. By sacrificing her own happiness and comfort, Martha exemplified genuine leadership when she loyally supported the American patriots and her husband's lengthy and dangerous absences.

Martha, true to her conviction, chose to maintain a joyful and content attitude to combat her loneliness and feelings of trepidation over her husband's possible death or conviction for treason. She wrote a friend saying, "To me that has never seen anything of war, the preparations are very terrible indeed, but I endeavor to keep my fears to myself as well as I can."

The American Revolution lasted a bloody and punishing eight years. Leaders step up and initiate change or do all they can to improve a poor situation when possible. Martha made it her business to improve the situation however she might, by visiting and caring for her husband and comforting his troops, between battles.

Leading by example, Martha reached out to enlist other women in the colonies to volunteer on behalf of the Continental Army. She was credited with the organization of sick wards for the wounded soldiers and praised for lifting the morale of her husband's undernourished, frostbitten and depleted troops.

Martha had seen enough sickness and death for two lifetimes, yet tragedy would again visit her home and heart. Her two remaining children would also pass away and Martha again provided evidence of her leadership when she and George adopted two of her youngest grandchildren to raise as their own.

Then at the age of fifty-eight, this loyal and fiercely private woman now faced eight demanding years under the glaring spotlight of public scrutiny. As democracy marched forward,

Martha was thrust into a new roll (with no title, no job description, no precedents) for which she was ill prepared.

With grace and decorum, Martha carried out the rigid rules of protocol laid out for her by President Washington's secretary. Far from her home at Mt. Vernon, she again felt lonely and often times "like a state prisoner." And *still*, Martha maintained: "I will not, however contemplate with too much regret disappoints that were inevitable." Martha's dedication and positive perspectives set the example and provided the role model for those who followed in her footsteps.

Martha is proof that we alone determine—by choice— our attitude in any given situation. No question, Martha could have acted sullen and felt resentful and downhearted. Yet she understood that our attitude and choices are more important than our past, our educational level, our finances, our failures or successes, our talents, and certainly our current circumstances. Leaders choose positive attitudes to maintain happiness and clarity of purpose.

REGARDLESS OF YOUR situation, your family life or any other supposed limitations, you have the power to improve your attitude. Without question, maintaining a positive attitude takes practice. However, it can be done and practicing that mind set enables us to see opportunity and possibility where there seemed to be none.

Positivity helps and supports every endeavor. Leaders understand this universal principle and practice implementing it everyday. To help develop a positive vision, set goals with daily achievable actions to reinforce favorable results. Train yourself and decide to use positive self-talk. The words we use, to ourselves as well as others, create our emotions and attitude.

Write down five things you are grateful for each day. Some days you may quickly come up with ten or more new ones; however, always list a minimum of five even if you have to repeat a few.

Choose to hang out with other positive friends and associates, remembering that attitude is contagious. Smile at everyone you come in contact with, and notice the positive responses you receive. You will feel better and so will they. Practice some form of physical fitness regularly, even if it is only twenty minutes of walking. When you do something constructive for your health, it makes you feel good and positive thoughts lead to a positive attitude.

I am not suggesting that you become a pom-pom wielding cheerleader who believes a positive attitude alone will solve all problems. When faced with a challenge, ask for advice; asking questions leads to solutions and helps us learn and grow.

With every situation in life, someone else has experienced those same obstacles, perhaps with even greater challenges and fewer opportunities; if they can succeed, surely you can!

"What is the difference between an obstacle and an opportunity? Our attitude towards it. Every opportunity has a difficulty, and every difficulty has an opportunity."

—J. Sidlow Baxter,
Theologian

"The greatest day in your life and mine is when we take total responsibility for our attitudes. That's the day we truly grow up."
—John C. Maxwell,
Leadership Author

"Our greatest freedom is the freedom to choose our attitude."
— Viktor E. Frankl,
M.D., Ph.D. and Holocaust Survivor

"Nothing can stop the man with the right mental attitude from achieving his goal; nothing on earth can help the man with the wrong mental attitude."
—Thomas Jefferson,
3rd President of the United States

2

LEADERS ARE
VISIONARIES

*"We are carried step by step to endure that
which we first think insupportable."*

—*Abigail Adams*

FOR YEARS, EXPERTS and universities have studied leadership and the qualities of top leaders around the world. In over 30,000 studies, all have concluded that "vision" is the most identifiable quality of a leader. Reviewing some of those studies and doing extensive research of my own, I have found several other commonalities that many experts agree on.

Visionaries are said to have vivid imaginations and the ability to clearly see a vision in their mind's eye that has not yet transpired or materialized. They are often described as individuals willing to experiment without deference to the views of existing authority. They purportedly have an unconventional nature that carries a sense of personal destiny, and is immune to social pressures and naysayers.

In addition to exuding confidence, visionaries are not worried about being liked and see themselves as victors over circumstances. They know where they are going, as opposed to focusing on where they have been. Visionaries are optimistic, with a purposeful behavior, and they never complain or explain. They have charisma, possess above-average communication skills to cultivate a partnership approach and are sensitive to others. Visionaries are said to have strong convictions, take calculated risks and reside in two worlds—the external world of what appears to be and an internal world of ideas, pictures, and thought.

Visionary leaders creatively choose where they want to be in the future and take the necessary steps to get there; they have a focused passion, the strength of will and knowledge of long-term goals and discipline. Visionary leaders believe in action and can articulate their dream to inspire others. If they also have integrity, strong core values and emotion, visionaries then have the ability to empower relationships, encourage loyalty and innovate change.

With optimism and high expectations, visionaries seek knowledge, personal growth and continuous learning opportunities for themselves and those around them. Visionaries are not threatened by subordinates, and they often have an uncommon openness and desire to encourage and support others who want to achieve and succeed. They organize and strategically plan ahead, typically delegating authority and refraining from micromanaging.

Visionary leaders have a purpose and direction with the brazen persistence to push through difficulties, misfortune, set backs and perceived failure. Visionaries take responsibility, focus on the solution and move towards progress instead of making excuses, criticizing others or feeling victimized.

Yes, visionary leaders do have a vision of the future and I want to emphasize not only a vision, but an action plan to generate its reality. One such revolutionary leader was Abigail Adams.

Had Abigail been born one hundred years after her birth in 1744, it would still be difficult to imagine a woman would write such things as, "It always seemed a most iniquitous scheme to me to fight ourselves for what we are robbing the Negroes of, who have as good a right to freedom as we have." Yet those were Abigail's exact words documented in letters to her spouse, John Adams.

Abigail clearly stated her position when she declared, "I will never consent to have our sex considered in an inferior point of light." Her belief was that equal rights included all people. Her insightful vision included education for all individuals as well, which was still an abstract concept during her lifetime. Abigail noted, for example, "Every assistance and advantage which can be procured is afforded to the Sons, whilst the daughters are wholly neglected in point of Literature."

As the country's Founding Fathers battled for independence, this visionary leader used her pen to address such an implausible transformation as, "If particular care and attention is not paid to the ladies, we are determined to foment a rebellion, and will not hold ourselves bound by any laws in which we have no voice, or representation."

In spite of the fact that Abigail's visionary dreams never materialized during her life time, she will always be remembered as "The First Lady of Liberty."

NOT EVERY VISIONARY is inspired to reshape the political and philosophical landscape of their country. Communities, places of work, worship, and home all need individuals who have a vision of improvement and who can inspire others to collectively achieve it.

Start with your personal interests or concerns. Begin by imagining that you have no limitations at all on what you can do. Be willing to explore your imagination and allow yourself to fantasize freely without restrictions. Before you can become a doer, you must first be a wishful thinker. Take the necessary time to contemplate alternatives to the current status quo. If you are only thinking one or two years forward, you are likely too rooted in today's reality which limits your perspective.

To achieve real visionary change, stay focused on the big picture and understand that you cannot reach your destination alone. You will need to convey a concise sense of purpose in order to attract the right people needed to achieve your dream. Look for those who are willing to try new things, who think more about the opportunities of tomorrow and less of the problems of the past.

Encourage your team to be creative, offer new ideas, and remain open to all avenues. Ignore naysayers and those who tell you something is unthinkable or unattainable. If you stay focused on the end result, as opposed to individual steps, you are more likely to connect the dots or find pieces and events that can be linked together to achieve your desired result.

When it comes to visionary changes at work, home or related to an organization you support, be prepared to take a hard look at what needs to be done and why. The answers can be found in asking questions. Depending on your business model, here are some examples:

- Where do we stand currently?
- Where do we need to go to be competitive?
- What needs to be done to get us there?
- What change would our customers most like to see?
- Where are our blind spots?
- What's working, what's not and why?
- What haven't we thought about?
- What do we not expect to see or have happen?

Unexpected opportunities are all around us, waiting to be discovered. It was Abraham Lincoln who recognized this and said, "No opportunity is ever lost, someone else will find it."

If you have ever thought, "There has to be a better way," then likely there is. Generally, the challenge is not in discovering the solution, but rather setting aside all the reasons something cannot be achieved. Write down anything and everything that would improve a situation, make it more equitable, more valuable, or more comfortable. Are the reasons meaningful, worthwhile, and/or important? If the answer is yes, then be the visionary who dreams the impossible, and make a commitment to attain the unthinkable.

—————

"The empires of the future are empires of the mind."

—Sir Winston Churchill,
British Prime Minister
(1940-1945 & 1951- 1955)

3

LEADERS
BUILD GOOD
RELATIONSHIPS

*"There is one secret, and that is the power we
all have in forming our own destinies."*

—Dolley Madison

I CANNOT THINK OF anything more profound than the
connections we have with other human beings. Beyond any
doubt, relationships are one of the most important aspects of
my life. Be it with family, friends, colleagues or acquaintances,
good relationships support and enhance one's existence.

Becoming a successful leader is virtually dependent
upon building relationships. The development of mutually
beneficial connections is a necessary and conscious decision.
In Dolley Madison's case, this attribute was clearly a natural

and heartfelt quality of her personality. Author and theologian Frederick Carl Buechner advises, "They may forget what you said, but they will never forget how you made them feel."

That precisely and literally characterizes Dolley Madison. She was referred to as "Hostess to the Nation," not simply because she was the nation's First Lady, but because she built genuine relationships with everyone with whom she came into contact.

She would look for something likable about every person she met, making her one of the most beloved First Ladies of all time. It was Dolley who forged the highly public role of a president's wife. It was she who established the stature and standard against which future First Ladies would be measured.

People, not politics, was what mattered most to her. She confirmed as much in a letter to her sister saying, "Politics is the business of men. I don't care what offices they may hold, or who supports them. I care only about the people." She believed the nation's citizenry was her constituency, as well as that of her husband. Putting individuals before and above politics earned her many followers and respect from both sides of the political aisle.

Dolley earned a reputation as a politically-savvy hostess, humanitarian and skilled diplomat. With warmth and sincere concern, Dolley marshaled in a new era of bipartisanship with discussions of compromise and conciliation, a bonafide endorsement of her leadership. According to one eyewitness, "Dolley strived to destroy rancorous feelings, then so bitter between Federalists and Republicans."

Many were quoted saying that Dolley was "all things to all men" and "you cannot discover who are her husband's friends or foes." So skilled at building good relationships, she was credited with winning her husband's (President James Madison) re-election bid, and earned the celebrity of "Presidentress."

Meanwhile, the president's opponents complained of having to run "against both Madisons." When Dolley resided in the White House, it was said to be "one of the few places in the nation where hope and determination continued to flourish."

Dolley's skills at building key relationships were so highly regarded that nearly thirty years after leaving the executive mansion, First Ladies and White House hostesses who succeeded her, continued to seek out Dolley's advice and guidance. As a tribute to her leadership, she was awarded an honorary seat in Congress.

When she passed away, Washington City honored her with the largest state funeral the capital had ever seen for a woman. Quoted in his eulogy to Dolley, President Zachary Taylor accurately predicted, "She will never be forgotten, because she was truly our First Lady for a half-century."

FOLLOW DOLLEY'S LEAD and look for something likable in every person you meet. Abraham Lincoln said it best, "I don't like that man. I must get to know him better." Learn to accept and celebrate differences. We are all unique and it is important we strive to see things from an inclusive point of view.

There are numerous ways to develop positive connections. Thinking about how you can serve others is a good start, acting on those thoughts builds substantial relationships. Offer assistance before and without being asked. Be generous with your time and attention. Make it your practice every day to do something nice for someone else. Real connections thrive when you do something for someone else, just because you can, without regard for what you may get in return.

Ask people about themselves and most importantly take the time to listen attentively. Active listening—when you paraphrase your understanding of what someone says and reflect it back for verification prior to responding—is the single most important listening skill to develop. Seek commonality. Be present and free of distraction. In today's technology-dependent world, our full attention is a precious commodity.

Regardless of how minor or fleeting it may be, every relationship has value. Practice understanding and empathy. Those who cultivate strong and lasting connections understand this and practice the universal rule, "Always respect and treat others the way you want to be treated." Seize every opportunity to cement existing relationships and cultivate new ones.

*"The most important single ingredient
in the formula of success is knowing how
to get along with people."*
—Theodore Roosevelt,
26th President of the United States

4

LEADERS ARE CONFIDENT

"...you have frequently endeavored to teach me fortitude. I knew not then how much I should need it." (in a letter to John Quincy Adams)

— Louisa Adams

I BELIEVE EVERYONE is a leader in some form or fashion, be it in their organization, their community or their home. Think of what you do on a daily basis. Are you a positive role model, trustworthy and acting with integrity? Do you support, motivate or influence others? Do you take charge of situations? Are you willing to serve others? All of these are characteristics of leaders.

The question is not whether or not you demonstrate any of those qualities, but rather, do you see yourself as a leader? That is a very important distinction! Leaders have the self-confidence needed to achieve their goals. Statistically over

90 percent of leaders report to someone else. You can still be a leader with your ideas, contribution and attitude. However, if you are unable to see yourself as having leadership qualities, you will miss opportunities to demonstrate your added value.

Louisa Adams, the only First Lady born outside of the United States, is an example of someone who allowed her insecurities to overshadow her natural leadership qualities. Louisa was well educated, spoke four languages and demonstrated talent as a musician, author and poet. Yet she refused to accept acknowledgement for her many achievements; instead, Louisa focused on another reality in her life, that being the prestigious family she married into. Her feelings of inferiority overwhelmed any sense of her strengths.

In a letter to her father-in-law, Louisa wrote in part, "The woman selected for your wife [Abigail Adams] was so highly gifted in mind, with powers so vast, and such quick and clear perception, altogether so superior to the general run of females, you have perhaps formed a too-enlarged opinion of the capacities of our sex..."

When Louisa met John Quincy Adams, he was already a mature diplomate working in her native England. John never hid the fact that his political career came before everything else in his life. Even when he told Louisa that he loved her, he added that he loved his country more.

John's father, John Adams, was the sitting second president of the United States. His mother Abigail, was the articulate and politically astute "First Lady of Liberty." If John's passion for patriotism and his family's political standing were not intimidating enough, it was inevitable that Louisa would one day be residing in America, living totally out of her element.

Raised in Europe as the daughter of a once wealthy businessman (who embarrassingly lost everything), Louisa had been presented at Royal European courts. Consequently that environment was comfortable and familiar. She was described as "an exceptional beauty, a gracious hostess, a brilliant conversationalist, and an extravagant, household manager." Sadly, life as the wife of a poorly paid traveling American diplomate was hardly royal. Louisa found her marriage and responsibilities burdensome and filled with unhappiness, making her depressed and miserable.

When in Washington Louisa impressed government figures with her political astuteness, made many friendships with her hospitable manner and entertained Washington society at elaborate dinners. Nonetheless, she lacked confidence in her abilities. She noted in her diary, "The more I bear, the more is expected to me (sic), and I sink in the efforts I make to answer such expectations."

Except Louisa was the only one who believed that she "sank in her efforts." She was praised for her gracious entertaining and captivated her guests when she recited her own poems or played the piano and harp. Historians describe Louisa as one of the leading ladies of Washington society during her era, and credit her social power as a benefit to her husband's political interests.

When she doubted her capabilities, it might have helped Louisa had she recalled her courageous journey through war torn Europe. When she lived in St. Petersburg, John summoned his wife and youngest son to meet him in Paris. This was a dangerous crossing, some 2,000-miles by carriage. It was the dead of winter during the horrifying Napoleonic War, and the travelers endured endless hazards and hardships. With resolve Louisa wrote, "From a proud and foolhardy spirit…," she decided to go on.

Louisa later noted in her diary, "Under all circumstances we must never desert ourselves," yet when she penned her memoirs, she titled it *Adventures of a Nobody.* Louisa would never know the admiration so many held for her. In order to attend her funeral, Congress adjourned as a tribute to the woman who believed she was a nobody.

IT IS SIMPLY a fact of life that someone will always have greater aptitude or talent than ourselves. Had Louisa been able to recognize and honor her strengths, she would have felt more confident. Unfortunately, Louisa was unaware that she could manage her thoughts to be more self-affirming.

Choose three people, known to you personally or not, that you admire. What qualities or attributes do you admire in them? If we notice something we aspire to be in someone else, that quality already lies within us—just waiting to be cultivated. Negative self judgements grow when you think there is nothing admirable about you. However, if you take the time to objectively look within yourself, you will come to realize that you have many admirable qualities. A sample handful of admirable qualities people admire includes: compassion, humor, loyalty, reliability, mannered, honest, broad-minded, curious, forgiving, patient; the possibilities are endless.

Find those qualities that apply to you and write them down in a journal titled My Admirable Qualities. When someone compliments you, practice responding with a simple 'thank you,' with no additional commentary. Add those comments in your journal as well. As you become more self-aware and acknowledge your admirable qualities, your old pattern of dwelling on negativity will diminish.

Everyone is good at something. Think about what you like to do, what you enjoy and what energizes you, everything counts. Now, associate a talent or skill that goes with your interests. Write those down in a Skills Journal, divided into existing skills and obtainable skills. Remember talents are natural and skills can be developed.

Finally, write down ten things you have achieved in an Achievement Journal, for example: produced the highest sales, received a promotion, completed a marathon, improved your health. Sustainable self confidence comes with accomplishing goals that you have set for yourself. Start with very small, achievable goals; for instance, stop chewing gum or substitute a glass of water for your third cup of coffee. Do not strive for perfection! Enjoy doing things successfully and well. Step by step you will begin to pile up your triumphs. Then wake up five minutes earlier everyday to celebrate and reread your journals. Add to them as you continue to gain awareness, achievements, and confidence.

Rome was not built in a day. It takes time, effort and patience to build confidence.

—⁓—

"Confidence comes from discipline and training."
—Robert Kiyosaki,
Author

"You gain strength, courage, and confidence by every experience in which you really stop to look fear in the face. You are able to say to yourself, 'I lived through this horror. I can take the next thing that comes along.'"

—Eleanor Roosevelt,
32nd First Lady of the United States

———

*"Confidence is contagious.
So is lack of confidence."*

—Vince Lombardi,
National Championship Football Coach

———

"Believe in yourself! Have faith in your abilities! Without a humble but reasonable confidence in your own powers you cannot be successful or happy."

—Norman Vincent Peale,
Minister, Author and Forefather of
Positive Thinking

5

LEADERS SHARE THE GLORY

"If I get to the White House, I will neither keep house, nor make butter...I always take a deep interest in state and national affairs."

—Sarah Polk

TRUE LEADERS RECOGNIZE early on that much more can be achieved collectively than individually. It only makes good sense. Putting together a winning team takes both time and effort; however, the productivity and accomplishment the team delivers is invaluable. Once in place, the fastest way for a leader to diminish the effectiveness of the team is to abandon them when a mistake is made.

Conversely, when people feel supported and recognized, they have a better attitude, self-esteem is promoted and further contribution is encouraged. It makes good sense for a leader to acknowledge and praise team members, individually and collectively, every time it is merited. The majority of employees take pride in—and want to do—good work; if not, they do not belong on your team. Therefore, when people are commended for doing a good job, it promotes security, adds motivation and drives high performance.

Strong leaders make employee recognition a priority, as it can ensure an overall climate of efficiency, competency and mastery. While all of those things contribute and are important to an organization's success, leaders share the glory for other reasons as well.

Leaders are confident in themselves and know the contributions they make. Leaders are secure in their maturity and give credit freely, recognizing the intrinsic contribution of each team member. A good leader models generosity of spirit, assists each team member in achieving their highest goals and becoming their best selves and accepts that personal accountability is a cornerstone of true leadership.

One such confident and mature leader was Sarah Polk, perhaps the most politically astute woman of her day! Well over a hundred years before President Harry Truman coined the phrase, "It is amazing what you can accomplish if you do not care who gets the credit," Sarah lived that principle daily.

She was born into a prominent family in 1803, that believed service was a priority and education was essential. Consequently, Sarah received extensive schooling, for a woman of her era, and showed early interest in governmental affairs.

After marrying James Polk, a newly-elected Senator, Sarah devoted her entire life to advancing her husband's political goals. She served as his official secretary, advisor, manager and confidante throughout Polk's entire political life, providing her a platform from which to build her leadership skills.

So important was Sarah to her husband's career that a Nashville newspaper called her a "membress of the Congress-elect [sic]." James acknowledged as much when he wrote, "None but Sarah knew so intimately my private affairs... She was politician, counselor, nurse and emotional resource." Sarah intuitively embodied the advice Abraham Lincoln offered many years later. "Don't worry when you are not recognized, but strive to be worthy of recognition."

Maintaining her focus on legislative topics, but understanding that politics was exclusively a male club, she would lead her conversions with, "Mr. Polk believes or Mr. Polk is confident..." If others shared her [purportedly Mr. Polk's] opinion, she freely gave them credit. If they were of a different opinion, Sarah would articulate her position, always careful to not offend.

Working behind the scenes, well read and informed, she was able to enjoy in-depth discussions on all forms of legislation with Congressmen on both sides of the aisle. A conversation with future president Franklin Pierce caused him to exclaim that he, "Preferred discussing politics with Mrs. Polk to any man!"

Leaders are ready when opportunity knocks, and Sarah was well prepared when Polk became the first "dark horse" candidate to win the presidency. As First Lady, Sarah continued her policy of generously giving recognition to others. Taking no credit for her heavily-attended weekly receptions and other social gatherings, she would praise and acknowledge the White House employees she had charged with organizing the event.

Sarah understood the best way to lead others was to be well informed, offer disagreement in a nonthreatening manner, and always give praise to others for their thoughts and efforts.

EVERYDAY WE INTERACT with people who need and are deserving of recognition for their constructive in-put, ideas and/or actions. In an office with colleagues, at home with family, or in casual interactions with others, positive acknowledgement is a simple, immediate and a powerful reinforcement that validates one's effort.

A sincere observation like, "Great job on the recent project," "I appreciate your caring customer service," or "Thank you for taking action on...," takes so little time and effort yet produces many rewards. You can write a simple note, send a quick email or leave a short phone message of thanks or appreciation. President William Howard Taft reminded us, "Failure to accord credit to anyone for what he may have done is a great weakness in any man."

Empower others by letting them know they are important. Today, we also have the ability to Tweet or post on LinkedIn an individual's accomplishment or performance, which in turn notifies others of their recognition. Get in the practice of noticing how everyone contributes and make a habit of acknowledging them. When you are looking for the favorable, it is easily found.

"Kind words can be short and easy to speak, but their echoes are endless."

—Mother Teresa,
Nobel Peace Prize recipient

6

LEADERS HAVE INTEGRITY

"If a contraband [runaway slave] is in Camp, don't let the 23rd Regiment (of which her husband was a Colonel) be disgraced by returning [him/her] or anything of the kind."

—*Lucy Hayes*

WHEN SOMEONE IS said to have integrity, what is the first thing that comes to mind? Most people might say honesty and that is correct in part. Integrity is *also* defined as "having and adhering to strong moral principles" as well as "the state of being whole or undivided."

Is it important for a leader to be honest? Of course; however, it is more important for a leader to have integrity. Leaders must live by strong principles and feel whole and undivided within. Consider wholeness as the consistency between what you say and what you do daily.

Principles not only focus your attention, you gain both assurance and become unconcerned with what others might think. Leaders lead by example and can empower every team member to commit, to become a guardian of the firm's ethics, if you will, and to maintain integrity with their customers and each other.

The earlier you establish moral principles, the more ingrained and crystal clear they become. That is not to say initial attitudes or perspectives cannot change, develop and grow. Depending upon where and how you grew up or who your childhood role models were, you can choose, as you mature, to honor new values. For Lucy Webb Hayes, she learned her values early.

Lucy's widowed and strongly-principled mother was raising three young children and facing poverty when she unexpectedly inherited over a dozen slaves. Mrs. Webb took in boarders and cleaned homes, declaring definitively, "I will take in washing to support my family before I would [sic] take money for the sale of a human being."

Years later, when Lucy was pregnant with her fourth child, it would have been easy for her to slip into a selfish mindset; however, her principles were powerful and clear. She supported her husband's (Rutherford B. Hayes) decision to leave his law practice and volunteer for what Lucy called a "holy and just cause" civil war.

Lucy also supported the temperance movement and continued the family's practice of serving no liquor in their home—even once they occupied the White House. Chided by senators, congressmen and other disappointed guests, who nicknamed her "Lemonade Lucy," she remained unmoved.

Lucy noted, "Without intending to be public, I find myself for a quiet mind-her-own-business woman rather notorious."

To improve and strengthen your integrity:
- Identify your intrinsic core values.
- Seek the best for others without regard for personal gain.
- Demonstrate pride in your company.
- Spend company funds and use resources wisely.
- Take responsibility.
- Put your company's needs above your own.

Leaders demonstrate integrity in several ways:
- They are consistent, have clear standards and live their principles.
- They support the team during both good and tough times.
- They serve others, expecting nothing in return.
- They do not pretend to know everything.
- They treat everyone with respect.
- They take ownership of their problems, accept mistakes and learn from them.
- They encourage others to express their point of view.
- They empower others to share concerns.
- They are willing to take risks and strive for excellence.
- They make a practice of using their free time wisely, as they are committed to achieving things of importance.

If you are looking to enter a college with limited openings, seeking employment, starting a new business, up for a promotion, or establishing a new client base, be the stand-out individual with the highest integrity.

———— *∞* ————

"Real integrity is doing the right thing, knowing that nobody's going to know whether you did it or not."

—Oprah Winfrey,
Talk Show Host, Producer, & Philanthropist

7

LEADERS VIEW FAILURE AS OPPORTUNITY

"Keep the [White] house as it is, we are coming back just four years from today."

—*Frances Cleveland*

LEADERS UNDERSTAND ALL of the important benefits and rewards that can be gained from failure. I say can because the most valuable experiences only come from learning why something did not succeed. Learning and understanding "the why" increases the chances of future success. When inventing the light bulb, Thomas Edison famously remarked, "I have not failed. I've just found 10,000 ways that won't work."

It was an observation President Calvin Coolidge perceived this way, "If I had permitted my failures, or what seemed to me at the time a lack of success, to discourage me, I cannot see any way in which I would ever have made progress." This affirms that, locked inside the failure is a new process, method or direction that was previously concealed.

Failure ultimately shapes a leader, as it teaches survival, how to manage adversity and reinvention. These powerful resources and experiences form a secure foundation for future success, what I like to call "astute ineffectiveness." It is the wisdom embedded within failure that makes a leader stronger, furnishes insights and perspective to assist oneself and others in achieving more. In the end, it is what you do with failure that defines one's character.

I cannot think of one successful individual who has not failed at some point. Many of these names and their achievements are known to us—inventors Thomas Edison, Orville and Wilbur Wright; notable geniuses Albert Einstein, Isaac Newton, Charles Darwin; business gurus Henry Ford, F. W. Woolworth, Bill Gates; political leaders Abraham Lincoln, Winston Churchill, Harry Truman; athletes Babe Ruth, Michael Jordan, Tom Landry; musicians Wolfgang Mozart, Ludwig van Beethoven, The Beatles; authors Emily Dickinson, Stephen King, J.K. Rowling; artists Vincent van Gogh, Claude Monet, Steven Spielberg; actors Lucille Ball, Charlie Chaplin, Harrison Ford; and billionaires Mark Cuban, Richard Branson, Oprah Winfrey—and they all failed before achieving success.

It is inconceivable where we would be and what we would have missed, had these leaders refused to—accept personal responsibility, make corrections and move forward—time and time again! As Winston Churchill defined it, "Success consists of going from failure to failure without loss of enthusiasm."

Take into consideration some of the additional benefits that failure offers:

- The opportunity to start fresh with improved knowledge.
- The appreciation for just how close you are to success.
- The awareness of customers' or clients' preferences.
- The knowledge of how others respond to or overcome challenges.
- The insight on who you can rely on.
- The empowerment to trust your gut more.
- The reinforcement that failure goes hand-in-hand with success and is not its opposite.
- The situation provides a favorable circumstance to showcase other leadership skills.

True leaders look at failure as a prerequisite to innovation. They encourage their team to push through their fears, take risks and think outside the box. As Mike Ditka, pro football Hall of Famer said, "Success isn't permanent and failure isn't fatal."

In the course of a lifetime, unless you never try anything new—ever, failure is inevitable at some point. While creative thinking and taking risks increases that probability considerably, leaders welcome the learning curve failure provides. With that said, when it comes to health and safety issues, a leader's perspective is entirely transformed. Extra caution, research and examination must be executed and leaders must grasp the gravity regarding those issues.

Once you have been embroiled in a project for a period of time, it can be refreshing to take the time to step back, regroup and reanalyze the situation. That opening came for Frances

Cleveland when her husband lost his bid for re-election. She understood that losing a battle does not mean you lost the war. Frances could have interrupted the electoral loss as a failure. Instead she saw it as an opportunity to learn from the mistakes that prevented her husband from winning and told the White House staff confidently, "We are coming back."

What is most impressive about Frances Cleveland was her youthful wisdom. The youngest First Lady (merely 21 years old), Frances had intuition and comprehension beyond her years. Four years to the day that Frances made her proclamation, she did in fact move back into the executive mansion. She would become the only First Lady to serve two nonconsecutive terms.

Nevertheless, had her husband (President Grover Cleveland) chosen not to run for another term, Frances's observation would have still been correct. As she also stated, "I have not had my life yet. It is all before me...." In other words, the election four years prior was not a failure but rather an opportunity for her life to first begin.

During her second tenure, Frances had other occasions to demonstrate leadership qualities. For example, against White House opposition, Frances hosted Saturday receptions for working women who could not visit during weekdays. With integrity and confidence she consistently presented herself as a positive role model.

WHEN FAILURE DOES occur, what next? The worse thing is to not learn from the experience. Exploring failure can be time consuming and costly, yet leaders view both as an investment. Consider Tom Watson's Jr. response to an employee who thought he was going to be fired for his costly failure, "Not at all, young man,' Mr. Watson went on to say, 'we have just spent a couple of million dollars educating you.'"

The best way to confront a failure is head-on. Admit your part and evaluate what went wrong and why. Identify what you could do better or differently. Ask your team for feedback. Determine if an error was made repeatedly. Was there something omitted from the plan? Did you ignore a gut feeling? What was over or underestimated? Could failure have been avoided?

Identify the lessons learned. Review the strengths and weaknesses of the project and discuss options with your team. Immediately create a revised plan of action informed by your new insights. Finally, what opportunities came about from this perceived failure? Keep in mind, Post-it notes might never have been developed, had the initial adhesive not been imperfect.

"I've missed more than 9000 shots in my career. I've lost almost 300 games. 26 times, I've been trusted to take the game winning shot and missed. I've failed over and over and over again in my life. And that is why I succeed."

—Michael Jordan,
National Basketball Hall of Fame

"Only those who dare to fail greatly can ever achieve greatly."

— Robert F. Kennedy,
Senator and U.S. Attorney General

"Success is the result of perfection, hard work, learning from failure, loyalty, and persistence."

—Colin Powell,
Four-star General and Secretary of State

"Far better is it to dare mighty things, to win glorious triumphs, even though checkered by failure... than to rank with those poor spirits who neither enjoy nor suffer much, because they live in a gray twilight that knows not victory nor defeat."

—Theodore Roosevelt,
26th President of the United States

8

LEADERS ARE PERSUADERS

"We have within ourselves the only element of destruction; our foes are from within, not without."

—*Caroline Harrison*

PERSUASION AND MANIPULATION are *not* the same thing. Manipulation has the distinction of taking advantage of someone or having self-serving motives. A manipulator will sometimes use a threat—such as taking something away or wielding some other type of power. A leader's intent is to always serve the greater good. Therefore when a leader uses influence through persuasion, they are enlisting cooperation that benefits the group. There is a shared goal, ending in a win-win situation, creating feelings of respect and trust.

It has been said manipulators are heard, while persuaders are believed. Persuasion, now more than ever, is the language of business leadership. Leaders use persuasion to communicate decisions that benefit both parties that may have an emotional impact. Caroline Harrison was a leader whose use of persuasion advanced the standards for women at the end of the 19th century.

Caroline, a talented artist and accomplished musician, believed strongly in women's education and professional opportunities. Highly educated, she graduated college in 1853. So appreciative for the educational opportunity and the financial assistance afforded her during her early years of marriage, Caroline made a point of paying those gifts forward. She consistently gave generously of her time, talent and money to many causes and charities.

During her White House years with President Benjamin Harrison, Caroline's interest in porcelain china merged with her art and made china painting popular. The Johns Hopkins Hospital needed to raise money for their school of medicine and knowing that the sale of artwork from the First Lady would be valuable, it was not long before the hospital called her for support.

In 1893, the First Lady used her persuasion skills to convince three of the four male physician trustees at Johns Hopkins Hospital of the benefit of admitting women on an equal basis with men into their medical school. If they agreed to that, she was happy to donate her beautiful hand-painted china for their cause. In addition, she agreed to host receptions and fund raisers to raise even more money for the hospital. Dr. William Henry Welch, the one dissenting trustee, later changed his view and wrote in part, "The necessity for coeducation in some form, becomes more evident the higher the character of the education. In no form of education is this more evident than in that of medicine ...we regard coeducation a success."

———*ooo*———

WHEN IMPLEMENTING PERSUASION in your approach, you will draw on some of your other leadership skills as well. Establish credibility by inviting discussion. Listen intently so you can understand how to incorporate compromises if necessary. People respond positively when their needs or concerns are actually heard and respected. A sincere, open mind strengthens trust. People are more likely to be open to persuasion from those they trust.

Energetic persuaders are successful because they believe in themselves and show enthusiasm for their subject matter. While these are important characteristics for a persuader, they are insufficient if you do not have total command, including any facts or figures, that may be involved in your proposal.

Persuasion requires persistence, it is a strategy, not an end result. Take caution that your persistence does not become a nuisance. Watch facial expressions and body language. If you see or feel annoyance from your audience, stop! Finally, show empathy by putting yourself in the other person's situation. Ask yourself, what is important to them and why should they follow your lead?

If in your mind's eye this feels too overwhelming to think about, you might want to consider the four essential components of persuasion.

- Present your solution, method or product in such a way that carries emotional appeal.
- Reinforce your position with motivating and picturesque language.
- Identify relatable advantages or benefits for the person or group.
- Offer compelling evidence using metaphors, examples, diagrams.

Emotionally charged stories are the most persuasive. In crafting your story, you may want to ask yourself: Does my proposal match my listener's emotion? Is there sufficient common ground that the listener can be open to receive my message? Have I included all of the benefits and evidence necessary to support my position?

———~ono~———

"To be persuasive we must be believable; to be believable we must be creditable; to be credible we must be truthful."

—Edward R. Murrow,
Journalist

9

LEADERS ARE
PRINCIPLED

*"If I could not have both I should choose my
children's respect rather than their love."*

—*Edith Roosevelt*

JUST AS THERE are different styles of leadership, leaders have
distinct principles by which they conduct their lives. It is their
personal truth that serves as a foundation for their beliefs,
behaviors and attitudes. Unlike things that are invented,
principles are personal, discovered and specific. It is these
principles that shape leaders lives and govern their objectives.

Strong leaders recognize that success requires flexibility
and continuous improvement. However, their personal moral
code is never compromised. Whereas facts can be learned,
be true or false and even forgotten, a code of values requires
no memorization. It is a leader's cornerstone, compass and
weathervane.

As people grow, their life experiences shape their values. Edith Roosevelt believed the same strict moral standards she learned as a child applied equally to both her sons and daughters.

An indispensable presence in Theodore Roosevelt's life, Edith was a practical, some would say frugal, financial manager with sound judgement. Moving into the White House challenged Edith's deeply rooted values; not spending money in ways she viewed as foolish and maintaining her children's privacy was paramount. Unwilling to give up her principles, the leader in Edith came up with creative solutions.

When ridiculed in the newspaper for spending too little on her clothes and looking as such, Edith accepted it with a sense of pride and saved the article in her scrap book. While entertaining, she set a budget and, if the White House staff began to run low on punch, she instructed them to put more ice cubes in the glasses. If the food ran out, she simply shrugged her shoulders and appeared indifferent.

To keep the press from clamoring for pictures of her children, Edith arranged for a professional photographer to take family photos. She then gladly offered these images, the quality of which she so carefully controlled, to anyone who asked.

According to an old proverb, 'blood is thicker than water.' According to Edith, values are thicker than blood. When Franklin Roosevelt (a distant cousin) ran for the presidency, Edith openly campaigned for his opponent. She could not support Franklin, not due to any bad blood between the families, but simply because her values were different from his.

—⁕—

DISCOVERING THE SKILLS of leadership is easy. While there are others, many are discussed in this book. What could take some time and effort is defining your core principles...the moral code that influences your underlying beliefs and guides your decisions.

Ask yourself, do you have convictions of your own or do you live by the consensus of others? Who do you respect, either living or deceased (a parent, teacher/coach, colleague, clergy, world leader) and why? What principles shaped and guided their lives?

Then I suggest you think through and write down your personal, non-negotiable code of principles. Do not try to impress others with your list, it is your personal reminder of how you want to conduct your life. Become the person others want to follow. Those who aspire to be leaders, must discern a very important difference between fame and greatness. Fame is The Beatles; greatness is Gandhi.

At the end of the day, the position is just a position, a title is just a title, and those things come and go. What is truly important is your values and personal essence.

—⁕—

"Change your opinions, keep to your principles; change your leaves, keep intact your roots."

—Victor Hugo,
Novelist

"I love those who can smile in trouble, who can gather strength from distress, and grow brave by reflection. 'Tis the business of little minds to shrink, but they whose heart is firm, and whose conscience approves their conduct, will pursue their principles unto death."
—Leonardo da Vinci,
Universal Genius and Great Painter

"Moral authority comes from following universal and timeless principles like honesty, integrity, treating people with respect."
—Stephen Covey,
Author

"A people that values its privileges above its principles soon loses both."
—Dwight D. Eisenhower,
34th President of the United States

10
LEADERS PLAN 5-10 YEARS AHEAD

"This (her husband's appointment as secretary of war) was much more pleasing to me than the offer of the Supreme Court appointment, because it was in line with the kind of work I wanted my husband to do, the kind of career I wanted for him and expected him to have."

—Helen Taft

ONE QUESTION OFTEN asked is, are five-ten year plans really necessary? The answer is yes. For businesses, with any hope of long-term success, it is a necessity. It strengthens a company's brand and reinforces the responsibility of paying attention to the competition.

It is equally important for individuals. It dramatically increase their chances for success both in business and their personal lives. One major misconception is that the time frame is too far into the future and so much is going to change, transpire and progress between now and then, why bother? First of all, five years is not that far away. It might sound like an eternity to a teenager waiting to get a driver's license or a student just starting college; however, looking back time flies rather quickly. If you believe nothing else, heed this universal truth, "The older you get, the faster time goes!"

Of course things will change and progress, that is why leaders review their plans and make adjustments regularly. You might discover that what you are working towards no longer meets your current lifestyle or desires. That is possible and not unusual, but without adjustments and a revised plan, you could remain stuck where you no longer want to be for another ten years!

Regardless of your current position, it took time and training to get where you are. It is only logical that auxiliary preparation will be necessary for a favorable transition, be it a new profession, business or vocation. If you have no idea where you want to be in five years, most likely you will not be happy or satisfied where aimless and indifferent winds sweep you.

Leaders understand the necessity for short, intermediate and long-term planning to fully develop goals, resources and timetables to achieve results. When implemented, planning supported with flexibility to adapt to unforeseeable circumstances, provides a solid sense of purpose, focus and motivation. To avoid disruption in employee management, succession planning is also a valuable tool to highlight vulnerabilities in an organization's continued growth.

Winston Churchill emphasized the phase "He who fails to plan is planning to fail" from Benjamin Franklin, scientist, inventor and diplomat, one of America's founding fathers.

Ten-year plans can be more challenging and also more rewarding. Helen Taft was a leader who took personal responsibility for her life. She made a commitment to the life she wanted and through long-term planning made that life a reality.

In 1877 Helen Taft confirmed, "Nothing in my life reaches the climax of human bliss I felt when, as a girl of sixteen, I was entertained at the White House." From that moment on, Helen made it her life's ambition to one day live in the executive mansion. However, thoughts of the White House and politics was simply unprecedented thinking when you examine the role and opportunities for women in the late 19th century.

Helen was intelligent and an independent thinker with a serious attitude and strong opinions, which she articulately defended. Had she been born a male, politics would have been a foregone conclusion. Although ambitious and determined, Helen understood all too well that her strong political desires were far beyond what women's suffrage could help her achieve. Women did not yet even have the right to vote, so the presidency for a female was simply out of the question.

Living in the White House could only be fulfilled by grooming the right spouse. So after marrying William Taft, a lawyer, Helen turned her doggedness in the direction of her husband's career opportunities. Planning years in advance, she began by making connections in high social circles to establish opportunities for future state and federal appointments.

It was Helen who persuaded her unwilling husband to accept the appointment of U.S. Solicitor General. Later, when she saw an opportunity outside of the United States—the governorship in the Philippine Islands—Helen revised her plan. Any anxiety she may have felt moving three young children to Manila was offset by the invaluable chief executive experience she knew her husband would gain.

Proving his ability in the Philippines, President Theodore Roosevelt offered Taft his ultimate career ambition, an appointment to the Supreme Court. Maneuvering her biddable husband to her desired career path, Helen most likely said HELL NO. (Maybe not in those exact words, but not unimaginable as Helen was known to swear on occasion, enjoy a cocktail and gamble at cards.) In her memoirs *Recollections of Full Years,* Helen wrote in part: "I had always been opposed to a judicial career for him (Taft)..."

Instead she pressured her husband into accepting the secretary of war post, despite its meager eight thousand dollar annual salary. Now positioned as a cabinet member, Helen campaigned vigorously for Taft to announce his candidacy for the presidency. She aggressively ran a one-woman crusade for President Roosevelt's endorsement. Helen was so assertive, the president himself "called Helen into his office to rebuke her on her unwomanly behavior." Distinguished First Lady historian Carl Sferrazza Anthony wrote: "A powerful incumbent president conferring with the wife of his potential successor was unprecedented in presidential history."

During her husband's campaign, Helen was Taft's coach and confidant advisor. Under her management, she suggested specific language to use in his speeches and how to position himself. There is absolutely no doubt that without Helen's galvanizing leadership skills, long-term planning and constant reassessment, Taft would never have become president.

Had Helen simply accepted the female Victorian values placed upon women of her era, the likelihood of her living in the White House would have been microscopic. Instead, she chose to embrace the only power available to her and in doing so, reached the pinnacle of her desires by carefully planning, preparing and adjusting years in advance.

INVEST IN YOURSELF and avoid having regrets twenty-five years from now. Writing a five-ten year plan will take significant effort and serious contemplation. With that said, you need not have all the answers, nor have your plan written within the next 24 hours. Creating a rewarding and enriched life is not only the greatest gift you can give yourself, it is your sole responsibility. Be successful at discovering your interests, talents and purpose. Jim Rohn reminds us that, "Success is nothing more than a few simple disciplines, practiced every day."

Begin by thinking of your life as a whole. Later you can separate out the various areas and construct sub-categories. What do you want for yourself regarding an occupation, income, travel, family and experiences? What type of life do you want to live? What is important to you and what activities energize you? What do you want to achieve, learn to do? What legacy do you want to leave, medical cure do you want to discover, or situation do you want to improve?

Write everything down that comes to mind. Determine which are near, intermediate and long-term desires. List the things that will need to occur, in order to achieve each one. Review and revise regularly. It is your life and it need only be significant to you. Begin building it today.

———❦———

"Success depends upon previous preparation, and without such preparation there is sure to be failure."
—Confucius,
Chinese Philosopher

11
LEADERS FOCUS ON THE MISSION

"The dear face opposite me was drawn and lined; as I sat there watching the dawn break slowly I felt that life would never be the same; that something had broken inside me; and from that hour on I would have to wear a mask— not only to the public but to the one I loved best in the world; for he must never know how ill he was, and I must carry on."

—Edith Wilson

BE IT A mission statement for a large corporation or personal declaration, identifying the mission is critical. It is a powerful tool that helps maintain focus, provides a path for success and clears away all distractions.

A businesses' mission statement defines its purpose and is the heart and clarifying reason for its existence. An organization with an explicit mission inspires employee dedication, improves performance by setting priorities and increases profitability by fostering customer loyalty.

The true value of a mission establishes the 'what and why' of an organization and sets its brand apart from its competitors. Mission-driven leaders in turn set performance goals, helping employees connect their work to the company's ultimate purpose.

Seventy years before Stephen Covey wrote the book, *The 7 Habits of Highly Successful People,* suggesting in part that you, "Begin with the end in mind," Edith Wilson was crystal clear on her mission—keeping her severely ill spouse (President Woodrow Wilson) alive. After he suffered a paralytic stroke, Edith understood the only thing preventing the president from certain decline was his burning desire and determination to see the League of Nations (later known as the United Nations) ratified by Congress.

Edith's personal conviction was supported by his doctors. The only thing keeping her spouse fighting to live, was for the president to remain in office. What became her life's purpose created a historical scenario, one that could never happen again. With the exception of the president's medical team, NO ONE—not the vice president, cabinet members, or members of congress—would be permitted to see or speak to the president for several weeks. All communication, paperwork and governmental business, went through Edith.

She was a leader who would not be dissuaded in her unambiguous mission: to keep her husband in office.

AN EXAMPLE OF a powerful mission statement from a successful, specialty grocery business reads: "The mission of Trader Joe's is to give our customers the best food and beverage values that they can find anywhere and to provide them with the information required to make informed buying decisions. We provide these with a dedication to the highest quality of customer satisfaction delivered with a sense of warmth, friendliness, fun, individual pride, and company spirit."

Just as businesses and corporations use a mission statement to define who they are and why they exist, a personal mission statement can bring purpose and focus to your daily life.

A personal mission statement should identify what is really important to you: clarify your deepest aspirations and define who you want to *become*. Author and branding consultant William Arruda, offers this template when writing your mission, "The value you create + who you're creating it for + the expected outcome."

Some helpful questions you will need to answer are: What do I want from my life? What am I passionate about? What are my values? What are my talents? Considering our complex lives and need for balance, you might consider writing separate mission statements for your career life, family life and community life.

The more personal and specific it is, the greater impact your statement will have. Sharing your mission with those in your life creates accountability. Reviewing your mission regularly will not only improve your life, it will help you be a better person, a better leader.

—◦◦◦—

"A mission statement is not something you write overnight...but fundamentally your mission statement becomes your constitution, the solid expression of your vision and values. It becomes the criterion."

—Stephen Covey,
Author

12
LEADERS CONTROL THEIR DESTINY

"I know what's best for the President. I put him in the White House. He does well when he listens to me and poorly when he does not."

—*Florence Harding*

DESTINY...DOES IT control us or do we control it? Some believe destiny is in control, whether we like it or not. After all, it is defined as a predetermined course of events. However, there are countless leaders who refuse to let fate control their future, they take responsibility for their choices and their destiny.

Consider the story of Nick Vujicic, a man born with a rare syndrome called Tetra-amelia—the absence of all four limbs. If anyone's fate was sealed at birth, it should have been Nick's. Despite what many would consider insurmountable obstacles, today Nick is a successful speaker, married to a beautiful woman and father of an adorable son. Should you find yourself wanting to have a pity party one day, do yourself a favor and view Nick's remarkable videos on line. He is a leader who continues to have command over his destiny.

Nando Parrado was one of the sixteen survivors of a plane crash in the Andes, where temperatures were -30 degrees below zero and there was no food for seventy-two days. Was he *destined* to survive the plane crash that took the lives of his mother and sister? Or was his survival dependent upon his tenacity and fortitude? According to Mr. Parrado, "It is better to decide and make a mistake than not to decide."

It was Jacqueline Kennedy who said, "Learning to accept what was unthinkable changes you." Florence Harding, who called the White House home forty-years before Jackie, accepted and made the most of what was unthinkable to her—becoming First Lady of the United States.

Independent and determined, Florence Harding began her adult life pregnant and unwed at nineteen. She was adamant about leaving her parent's home and humiliating her wealthy, tyrannical and emotionally-abusive father. Just two years after eloping with her alcoholic husband, Florence found herself abandoned in a 'small furnished room' with no money and no food to feed her two year old infant. Her father, who had cut off all contact with his daughter, now refused her pleas for assistance. Although there is much more to the story, Florence persevered and developed into a leader of her own creation.

Years later, Florence married Warren Harding who owned and published the *Marion Star* newspaper. It was not long before Florence took over the management and operations of the business. She started running Harding's business and later his life, it was Florence who was the driving force behind her husband becoming president.

Florence was comfortable with the national press. She helped craft a favorable public image for both herself and the future president. As a feminist, she saw women's suffrage a foregone conclusion and was the first wife to cast a vote for her presidential spouse. During Harding's inaugural speech, Florence could be seen mouthing the words as the President spoke.

Arriving at the White House for the first time, Florence was widely reported to say, "Well, Warren Harding I got you the Presidency. Now what are you going to do?" An integral part of the administration, she instructed potential appointees to send information for the president through her. Florence not only weighed in on Cabinet appointments, she was responsible for the appointment of several women to various posts in government. The president frequently consulted with his wife on all political decisions.

She and President Harding were not party to the massive corruption quickly metastasizing throughout his Administration. As they became aware, Florence jumped into action in a last minute attempt to save her husband's legacy— albeit unsuccessfully. As scandals began to break and with the presidency crumbling beneath their feet, President Harding suddenly passed away.

LOOKING AT THE other side, some of the world's greatest leaders believe they were in some way instruments of destiny.

If you do believe in destiny, I encourage you embrace the idea that destiny favors those who are prepared. Chart a course and incorporate the leadership skills in this book. According to Seneca, a Roman philosopher (ca. 4 BC – 65 AD) wrote, "Luck is what happens when preparation meets opportunity."

Undeniably there will be circumstances you cannot control, but you can always control how you respond in any circumstance. Victor or victim? It is your choice. Take control of your destiny by discovering who you are. What are you here to do? Who are you here to serve?

"Destiny is no matter of chance. It is a matter of choice. It is not a thing to be waited for, it is a thing to be achieved."

—William Jennings Bryan,
Secretary of State (1913 – 1915)

13

Leaders Are Undaunted

"The independent girl is a person before whose wrath only the most rash dare stand, and, they, it must be confessed, with much fear and trembling."

—*Lou Hoover*

PARTICULARLY IN THE 21st century, with its many electronic advancements, it is as important for a leader to be as resolute in business as on the battlefield. Though the land mines may look different; they are equally as explosive and both generate fear in the person interacting with them.

Today's leaders need to have the acumen and agility to make quick decisions with conviction, decisions that significantly alter the course and potential outcome of the task at hand. This requires courageously confronting reality head-on and seeking feedback regarding any blind spots the leader may have. Winston Churchill, widely regarded as one of the greatest wartime leaders of the 20th century, spoke of it this way, "Courage is what it takes to stand up and speak; courage is *also* what it takes to sit down and listen."

The undaunted leader says what needs to be said and not what the team wants to hear; they value constructive dissent. Deferential debate reinforces the team's strength, and often it produces the most creative outcome.

Does one have to be unconventional to be an undaunted leader? No, and there was nothing conventional about Lou Hoover. Born in the 19th century, with a man's first name, Lou was the first female to earn a bachelor's degree in geology from Stanford University, where she met her spouse Herbert Hoover.

She exemplified undaunted leadership throughout her life. Lou was an intelligent, determined and independent woman who held high standards and expected everyone else to do the same. A world traveler who circled the globe more than once, Lou spoke five languages including Mandarin Chinese. She witnessed the boxer rebellion in China and immediately went into action by organizing assistance for the survivors. Once, while riding her bike to help feed and care for those in need, a bullet obviously intended for her, struck her bicycle tire; while it delayed her, she was undeterred in her mission.

First Lady during The Great Stock Market Crash and The Great Depression, Lou Hoover adamantly encouraged all Americans to follow her lead with charitable endeavors and volunteerism. Her belief was if everybody helped, there would be plenty of food and clothing for all. During her regular radio broadcasts Lou beseeched, "My plea is that our most important duty is to find when, how, and where people need help."

She was an early feminist who believed in racial equality. Despite knowing there would be vicious political repercussions from white segregationists, Lou extended an invitation to a black woman to join her for tea at the White House. Resolute in her decisions and unwilling to compromise her principles, she also refused to sign a real estate contract forbidding purchases from African-Americans or Jews. Lou Hoover was an undaunted, courageous leader, earning her the respect of the nation.

JUST AS LEADERSHIP skills can be learned, building the courage to be undaunted is also achievable. Think of it like strengthening a muscle. Over time, with the proper tools and practice, you can increase your muscle strength and tone your body. The more you master the tools in this book and gain experience, your courage will also grow and strengthen.

Be mindful that it is still important to connect and interact with others, even when you do not have all the answers. Stay in contact and communicate frequently, with your team and clients, without equivocation. At times it might feel uncomfortable, particularly if conflict is involved. Work through the uneasiness and have the conversation anyway. Set the example that you are not one to simply sit on the sidelines waiting for the storm to pass.

Be truthful and share the information you do know. Bear in mind, there is no shame in saying, 'I don't know.' Allow your humility to be greater than your ego.

It is important to make decisions and move forward. Give credit to others. Good leaders take less than their fair share of the credit and more than their fair share of the blame. Model holding yourself responsible and expect others to do the same.

No matter the obstacle (or size of the land mine), the undaunted leader meets the problem head on. Leaders remain determined to find solutions, a new direction, an opening where there seems to be none.

—⁓⁓⁓—

"A leader, once convinced a particular course of action is the right one, must have the determination to stick with it and be undaunted when the going gets tough."

—Ronald Reagan,
40th President of the United States

14

LEADERS GROW
MORE LEADERS

*"Great minds discuss ideas. Average minds
discuss events. Small minds discuss people."*

—*Eleanor Roosevelt*

THROUGHOUT THIS BOOK, I have discussed the various
qualities that make a leader. Universally, every leader has his
or her own style, personality and approach. What works for
one leader may not necessarily work for another. The more
one develops the qualities and skills of leadership, the stronger
that leader will be.

A commonly held belief is that you need only have followers
to be a leader. I disagree. Managers have followers who comply
with, emulate and succeed them. Skilled and valuable to the
organization though they may be, not all are leaders. Warren
Bennis, scholar, author and widely regarded as a pioneer in the

field of leadership studies determined, "Failing organizations are usually over-managed and under-led."

The truth is, the greatest leaders not only have a vision and inspire others to accomplish that vision, they also cultivate and grow other leaders. Gandhi, Martin Luther King, Jr. and Nelson Mandela, for example, all worked at educating and elevating other leaders to fulfill their dreams of a better world. They focused on the bigger picture, being and living the positive solution otherwise known as "walking their talk." By living their values and demonstrating the proper model, they sought to teach others to do the same.

The fate of an organization with only one leader, is to remain forever small. It was Myles Munrow, speaker, preacher and author who said in part, "True leaders invest in people. Because success without a successor is failure. So your legacy should not be in buildings, programs, or projects; your legacy must be in people."

Eleanor Roosevelt, voted The World's Most Admired Woman for eleven consecutive years, earned the nickname Eleanor Everywhere. Her objectives were ambitious, always driven by the desire to be of service.

She was a tireless, present and an accessible advocate for social and humanitarian causes around the globe. Eleanor was a world leader who propagated and nurtured hundreds of leaders during her lifetime as she continues to generations later.

In 1894, before the age of ten, Eleanor was orphaned. She was taken in by her grandmother, who made sure she would be raised with all of the proper graces and social etiquette expected of a New York debutante. However, instead of festive soirees, Eleanor was drawn to social activism and political reform.

History refers to the period of time between the 1890s and the1920s as the Progressive Era. The progressive movement was focused on eliminating corruption in government, while women's groups across the United States were organizing in full force on behalf of social reform. Topics such as prohibition, suffrage, school issues and public health were of major concern.

Eleanor was immediately drawn to the plight of those individuals from a very different socio-economic world than her own, the impoverished masses who lived and worked in deplorable conditions. It was during this time Eleanor's liberal opinions and biases began to evolve. With other like-minded debutantes she learned the power of organized political reform and its necessity to legally effect change. This group of women formally organized and called itself the "Junior League."

For the remainder of her life, while married to Franklin D. Roosevelt and long after his death, Eleanor devoted herself to innumerable campaigns. She was an early and constant champion for american workers, the poor, the young, women and civil rights.

Through each endeavor, Eleanor recognized the need to continually build and grow leaders who would carry the torch for the causes to which she was so deeply committed. In her unrelenting advocacy for those working in dangerous and unhealthy conditions, living in overcrowded tenement apartments, servicemen with mental health problems, impoverished immigrant children, fair wages and labor practices, or broadening education opportunities for the working-class, she knew a pipeline of leadership was required to see the fight through to the end.

Eleanor worked with and served on endless boards until new leaders were groomed and ready to join or replace her. A very small list of her affiliations includes: The National Consumer's League, The Women's Trade Union League, The League of Women Voters, World Peace Movement, American Red Cross, and National Association for the Advancement of Colored People (NAACP).

One of Eleanor's proudest achievements and possibly her most enduring legacy came when she was appointed delegate to the United Nations. As chairwoman for the Human Rights Commission, she helped draft and pass the Universal Declaration of Human Rights, the first global expression of rights to which all human beings are inherently entitled.

Hailed as one of the most influential American women of the 20th century, it is clear why President Truman called Eleanor, "The Worlds First Lady."

TO ENSURE YOU are a leader of business transformation and continued growth, you must develop and maintain a pipeline of skilled, prepared *future* leaders. To begin, you must learn how to allocate the time to assist and train others on how to perform successfully. In essence you are shifting from doing the work to teaching others how to produce results.

Embrace the theory that if you, "Give a man a fish, you feed him for a day; teach him how to fish and you feed him for a lifetime."

Empower potential leaders to have command of an assignment with little interference. Provide them with the instruction and tools to climb mountains bigger than they can summit alone. Make the task greater than one individual can fulfill, authorizing the person to choose teammates. Set a due date that feels earlier than expected; then get out of their way.

Be available to brainstorm solutions if asked. Listen attentively with the objective being to understand, more than to provide answers. Ultimately it is *always* the leaders responsibility. Regardless of the results, strong leaders accept any blame and give any credit to the team. The leader's role is to continually challenge capability and acknowledge effort.

As a leader who grows future leaders, you are the planner and coach, divested of the actual task. Your ability to read people and build strong relationships will assist you in differentiating those who can do the work from those who can lead the work. Not everyone wants to be captain.

> *"The function of leadership is to produce more leaders, not more followers."*
>
> —Ralph Nader,
> Author and Political Activist

"A leader is someone who steps back from the entire system and tries to build a more collaborative, more innovative system that will work over the long term."
—Robert Reich,
Professor, Author and Secretary of Labor

"Today, no leader can afford to be indifferent to the challenge of engaging employees in the work of creating the future. Engagement may have been optional in the past, but it's pretty much the whole game today."
—Dr. Gary Hamel,
Management Expert

"As a leader, I am tough on myself and I raise the standard for everybody; however, I am very caring because I want people to excel at what they are doing so that they can aspire to be me in the future."
—Indra Nooyi,
Businesswoman, Chairperson and Chief
Executive Officer of PepsiCo

15
LEADERS LEAD WITHOUT TITLES

"I am perfectly satisfied to be known as a housewife."

—*Mamie Eisenhower*

ARE TITLES REALLY necessary or even important? Necessary, absolutely not! Important? Titles do establish the chain of command but may or may not contribute to running an organization more smoothly. It is *everyone's* opportunity and responsibility to show leadership at their skill and position. A job is only a job, when it is viewed as such. We all have the ability to influence others, regardless of the title or position we hold. It is leaders who speak up and look for ways to benefit the greater good, thinking beyond their individual role.

Regardless of where someone is on the road to proficiency, be the leader who is ready and willing to assist them in achieving their best. Strengthening positions at every level is a win for the individual, the team, the organization and the customers they serve.

Mamie Eisenhower was a leader perfectly comfortable with the title of housewife. She had confidence in her abilities and was proud of the designation, as she recognized the significance and enormous responsibilities associated with the position.

Like all leaders, Mamie grew into the position. She had a spoiled and indulged childhood, whereby her mother advised her, "If you don't learn to cook, no one will ask you to do it." Mamie did learn, however, to run a household with servants and manage domestic finances proficiently.

These abilities were of no use to her as a young bride living on her lieutenant husband's (Dwight D. Eisenhower) $141.67 monthly salary. Mamie soon learned the many sacrifices military families have to endure, not the least of which being loneliness. There were a number of very lean years, with multiple moves. Some of the posts meant sleeping on army cots in very dilapidated quarters. It was during these difficult years that Mamie assimilated her many leadership skills. She shifted her attitude and fully accepted responsibility for the life she had chosen.

Mamie became a positive role model for other army wives. She built strong personal relationships, was a person of integrity and strived for excellence in all of her endeavors. A clear and straightforward communicator, Mamie never wavered from her principles.

While living in the White House, Mamie ran the executive mansion like a five star general, earning respect from both her staff as well as her husband.

SHOULD YOU BE seeking a particular title or position, here are some surefire ways to achieve it. To begin with, lead yourself. Leaders accept responsibility and claim their potential in all areas of their lives. Discard any behavior, situation or friendship that compromises you.

Step outside of your comfort zone. It is outside of your comfort where growth occurs and confidence increases. Understand the doubts you may have are based on nothing more than the lies that your fears have sold you. Or, as James Malinchak, business coach and speaker characterizes it, "FEAR stands for False Evidence that Appears Real."

Do not wait for the energy to "show up" that you perceive will be needed for a task. It is the task that will give you energy. Dedicate part of your leisure time to studying the lives of leaders you admire. Make self-care a priority through exercise and, most importantly, getting enough sleep. You cannot lead effectively if you feel physically depleted.

Remember, a title is only as good as the leader who holds it. It is not the designation but rather the influence you have and you can influence others from where you are right now.

"Leadership is an art expressed by the demonstration of characters worthy of imitation, emulation and inspiration. It is neither a title nor a position."

— Israelmore Ayivor,
Youth Leadership Coach & Author

"Leadership is not about a title or a designation. It's about impact, influence and inspiration. Impact involves getting results, influence is about spreading the passion you have for your work, and you have to inspire team-mates and customers."

—Robin S. Sharma,
Author and Leadership Expert

———❧❧❧———

"In the past a leader was a boss. Today's leaders must be partners with their people... they no longer can lead solely based on positional power."

—Ken Blanchard,
Author, Management Expert

———❧❧❧———

"Leadership is not about titles, positions or flowcharts. It is about one life influencing another."

—John C. Maxwell,
Leadership Author

16

LEADERS STRIVE FOR EXCELLENCE

"One man can make a difference and every man should try."

—Jacqueline Kennedy

EXCELLENCE IS THAT elusive quality of being outstanding that all good leaders strive to achieve, knowing there is always room for improvement. The Navy SEALs are arguably the best in the world at what they do and in part that excellence is a direct correlation to their dedication to relentless training and extensive preparation. The SEALs training template is an excellent model of striving for excellence.

In the Special Operations environment, people get the job done at all costs, knowing how to figure it out and make it happen. When an entire team thinks and acts this way, the bar on excellence is continually raised.

Good leaders are serious about what training can and should mean—being good is not good enough. An overwhelming majority of leading businesses and professional enterprises adhere to this philosophy. They do not simply want to enhance capability, but rather transform potential and proficiency.

In addition to world-class training, organizations that promote excellence have the courage to reposition those who will not or cannot step up. A training program that focuses on enhancing skills as well as bettering relationships throughout the organization is the ultimate goal.

Successful training must be dynamic, open and innovative. Continual learning is essential for everyone, including those doing temporary work and part-time employees. Not to be minimized is the feedback from those employees on the frontline, dealing directly with the organization's clients and customers. A wealth of information can come from multiple sources, none of which should be overlooked.

Jacqueline Kennedy was a hands-on leader who sought and practiced excellence in everything she touched. When Jackie was determined to restore original White House furnishings and turn the executive mansion into a world-class museum, no detail was too small to merit her attention.

She recruited a team of dedicated advisors and experts and clearly articulated her mission. Carefully crafting a plan, Mrs. John F. Kennedy (who disliked the title First Lady, saying it sounded like a saddle horse) listened to ideas and successfully helped create the White House Historical Association. Today, a White House curator continues to protect the historical integrity of the mansion.

When Jackie wanted to have the only state dinner held at George Washington's home, naysayers said it *could not* be done. The obstacles were insurmountable. One hundred thirty-eight guests, in formal black tie, needed to be transported from the White House to the Potomac, then down the river in boats, only to arrive on Mount Vernon's mosquito laden sloping lawn, with no rest rooms and no kitchen for the White House Chef to prepare the food!

The First Lady was undeterred. With her leadership and meticulous attention to every preparatory detail, fifty years later the dinner and historical event is still remembered as a glamorous and glorious success.

Carey Lohrenz, the first female F-14 Tomcat Fighter Pilot in the U.S. Navy, resonated with Jackie Kennedy's leadership style. Lt. Lohrenz defined "fearless" leadership in terms of: Prepare, Perform, Prevail.

LEADERS UNDERSTAND THAT meeting the objective requires preparation. In the preparation stage, you draft a detailed plan, review all possible contingencies and insure the objectives are clear to your entire team. You can NEVER over prepare. This is the time you review your mission's goals, what challenges you might encounter and what contingencies you may need to implement. Determine what role each team member will play and encourage feedback from the team.

Only after you are completely prepared do you begin execution. Adhere to your plan. Keep lines of communication open. To achieve excellence requires a crucial third step: debrief by bringing your team together to analyze how things went, and consider how it could have improved.

It is imperative for you as a leader that both you and your team continue to learn, stretch and improve. By debriefing, you can identify opportunities to improve the team's agility, ability to stay ahead of the competition and insure the best possible execution for future projects. Everyone that was involved in the first two phases should participate in this vital step.

If your goal is to build a culture of excellence, each team member needs to know their part is critical to the whole. When everyone is focused on excellence, synergies occur that vastly increase the probability of success.

———————

"We are what we repeatedly do. Excellence, then, is not an act but a habit."

—Aristotle,
Greek Philosopher

17

LEADERS ARE RESPONSIBLE

"Success has many faces; it need not be circumscribed by a title, a job [or] a cause. Success is not always 'getting.' It is more often 'giving.' It does not consist of what we do, but rather in what we are. Success is not always an accomplishment. It can be a state of mind."

—Lady Bird Johnson

I BELIEVE LEADERSHIP is the *essence* of responsibility. Just as you don't "do" leadership, you *are* leadership—responsibility is not something you have, but rather something that you are. Ultimately and rightfully, leaders are responsible for everything their team does and/or fails to do. Harry Truman acknowledged this precept with a sign on his desk that read: "The Buck Stops Here."

Leaders can and should delegate authority, but can never nor should they ever delegate responsibility. By modeling the acceptance of responsibility, leaders can instill this principle in their team.

A responsible leader is someone who embodies character, accountability, focus, confidence and courage. If that sounds like enormous shoes to fill, it is because they are. Such leaders get the job done and respond with, "What can I do" as opposed to, "That's not my department." Responsible leaders earn respect. Within their organization they promote a sense of partnership that benefits every part of the company including, of course, the fiscal bottom line.

The responsible mindset engages with people at a deeper emotional level and for the greater good. The responsible mindset promotes conscientiousness, a dedication to exceeding expectations and insists upon doing the right thing *and* doing things right.

Being accountable for what you say and what you do, on a timely basis, is being responsible. With responsibility comes the importance of prioritizing, as time is a precious resource. It is finite and irreplaceable, therefore the allocation of time is critical to what you can achieve.

In the face of crisis, there is no time for debate or delay: responsible leaders quickly and simply step up. Such was the situation with Lady Bird Johnson. A tragic turn of events thrust Mrs. Johnson on to the world stage, and she was expected to *immediately* demonstrate her effectiveness as a leader.

No one was prepared for what occurred that November day in 1963. A beloved president was assassinated and when the shock and horror began to subside, the country's eyes diverted from his beautiful young widow to her successor. Known only by her nickname, Lady Bird was a true southern lady, whose larger than life, intimidating and dominating spouse, Lyndon Johnson, referred to her simply as 'Bird.'

Lady Bird was already an experienced leader. The vice president's wife, gracefully accepted any job or challenge that came her way. She had been a frequent proxy for the First Lady and sought friendships across political differences. Any doubt that someone affectionally called Bird could possibly be a responsible leader was erased forever by a moment in time and the days that followed.

Her focus was crystal clear. The country was in turmoil, requiring strength, direction and compassion. When faced with angry crowds of dissidents, she exhibited courage and respect. When it came to constructive criticism of her husband's speeches, Lady Bird did not shy away from saying something unfavorable, yet it was done with encouragement and positivity.

TO DEVELOP THE principle of responsibility, be the first to show up and the last to leave. Accept every opportunity regardless of its size, including the most insignificant, and commit your best effort. Take the initiative and learn the duties of your immediate supervisor. Be prepared to stand in or assume the assignment.

Assume a higher level of accountability for your company's success by taking action when something needs to be done, before being asked. Know the business and think like an owner. Fulfill your commitments, carefully stewarding people, time and assets.

Cross departmental divisions to assist with projects, over and above your regular workload. Be dependable, accountable and incorruptible. Replace the politics of division with the politics of coalition that emphasizes a commitment to the common good.

"Accept responsibility for your life. Know that it is you who will get you where you want to go, no one else."

—Les Brown,
Author, Speaker,
House of Representatives (1977 – 1983)

18

LEADERS ARE WILLING TO SERVE

"Our success as a nation depends upon our willingness to give generously of ourselves for the welfare and enrichment of the lives of others."

—*Pat Nixon*

SEVERAL CHARACTERISTICS, PRACTICED regularly, determine a leader's effectiveness. If you compared various successful leaders, it is not uncommon that some will have greater strength in one particular attribute, while others may have mastered more of the overall essential qualities. I personally believe there is one golden rule that defines and clarifies leadership and that is *service to others*. You cannot be a leader without the willingness to serve.

President Kennedy encouraged Americans to serve both locally and globally when he said, "Ask not what your country can do for you, ask *what you can do* for your country." There are a number of ways a leader can serve. Pat Nixon chose volunteering and she lead by example with her commitment to others.

As First Lady, to enlist thousands of volunteers, Pat encouraged a national recruitment program to support a variety of community services. Not only did their communities benefit, there was a positive mental and physical impact on the volunteers. She supported the National Center for Voluntary Action and championed passage of the Domestic Services Volunteer Act of 1970.

Sitting quietly on the sidelines was never her style. Pat endorsed the Equal Rights Amendment and publicly divulged her pro-choice view on abortion, both very sensitive and controversial topics to this day. Furthermore, she served the visually, hearing and physically impaired, by insisting the White House be made easily accessible to disabled visitors.

It was commonly known that Pat Nixon did not like the world of politics. The intrusion of the press into her family's private life felt incessant, which caused her great emotional distress. Yet she soldiered on, leading others.

The assumption that she was in any way artificial or insincere, as her nickname Plastic Pat implied, was totally false! The truth is, although she had once performed as a local theater actor (where she met her husband Richard Nixon), standing in the limelight caused her to freeze stiff. Outside of camera range, Pat was admired for her warmth and geniality.

A dedicated and hard worker her entire life, Pat held the record as the most world-traveled First Lady, until another former First Lady Hillary Clinton's historic travels as Secretary of State. As the wife of the vice president and later president, Pat accompanied her husband to fifty-three countries around the world. She was given the unique diplomatic status of "Personal Representative of the President."

During every trip she minimized her formal events, preferring to visit orphanages, senior citizen centers, schools and hospitals. After a devastating earthquake in Peru that left 160,000 Peruvians homeless, Pat lead a major volunteer humanitarian effort and then accompanied ten tons of donated food, clothing and medical supplies to the country.

Given the opportunity and platform afforded the First Lady, Pat Nixon's ego could easily have been inflated, but it was not. She understood that leading others was an earned privilege, not a right. Therefore, she continually worked to serve her country by leading through example and not from a place of self-importance.

REGARDLESS OF WHO you lead—colleagues, clients, team members, family or a country—recognize that leading others is an honor and to do so effectively you will need to earn their respect. A proven way to do this is by acknowledging everyone's value and contribution.

Because actions override anything you say, always model exemplary behavior. Words that align with actions create trust, confidence and credibility. An example of a way to be of service to one's investors is to volunteer as a board member of a charity they are involved in.

Serve employees by helping them be the best version of themselves. Provide the resources, tools and support they need to preform their job well. Do not do their job, but rather help them figure out solutions and assist them in correcting mistakes. When you inspire people to feel fully engaged as a valued team member, you have served them well. Engagement energizes effort.

There are limitless opportunities to serve where you can truly make a difference and impact lives. Mentor others, outside of your work, so they too can be successful. Volunteer where you have a passionate connection: a cancer center, hospital, animal shelter, school, charity or senior center. Volunteering is as important to the volunteer, as it is meaningful to the institution.

In 2012, researchers from Wharton University of Pennsylvania, Yale's School of Management along with Harvard Business School conducted a study on volunteering. They found that people who invest time serving others feel a sense of effectiveness, productiveness and it feels like they have more time themselves! Astoundingly, spending as little as ten minutes a day helping others, you can feel less "time-constrained." Although no one has more than 24 hours in any given day, according to Professor Cassie Mogilner, the research demonstrated that, "People's subjective sense of time affluence can be increased."

Knowing you have made a difference is energizing. You can measure your service to others by answering the following questions: What impact did I have today? Was I a good role model? Where those whom I served encouraged to be more autonomous, more likely to serve others?

"The thing that lies at the foundation of positive change, the way I see it, is service to a fellow human being."

—Lee Iacocca,
CEO of Chrysler (1978 – 1992)

19

LEADERS COMMUNICATE EFFECTIVELY

"You give back, you don't give up."

—Betty Ford

FROM THE MOMENT we are born, we receive countless indications that tell us the world revolves around us. When we are hungry, we get fed; when we are wet, we get changed, and frequently when we cry, we get what we want. Even when we learn to speak, our vocabulary and delivery revolves around ourselves, not the person we are speaking with.

However, to communicate effectively, communication is about meeting the needs of others—not ourselves. Great leaders have learned the subtle and powerful elements of communication. They cultivate the ability to speak to their audiences emotions and aspirations. Words do matter. As Mark Twain put it, "The difference between the right word and the almost right word is the difference between lightning and the lightning bug."

Betty Ford, the only First Lady whose husband (Gerald Ford) was not previously elected vice president or president, was a compelling communicator. She never evaded the truth and she understood that her words could help others. Betty was a brave leader who spoke candidly, listened earnestly and when it came to health issues, made a difference in thousands of women lives, as you will soon discover.

A breath of fresh air, particularly in politics, Betty addressed all issues head-on, ignoring political correctness or personal embarrassment. She was a strong supporter of legalized abortion and fought tirelessly for the Equal Rights Amendment in the face of direct criticism from right-wing members of her own political party. It was the first time in history that a First Lady was picketed in front of the White House for her political opinion.

When asked on national television her opinion regarding pre-marital sex, marijuana, abortion, and her own psychiatric treatment, Betty was forthcoming on all fronts. A large percentage of the country disagreed with her personal views, causing her husband to remark in jest, "[Betty] just cost him 20 million votes." Nevertheless, a greater percentage praised and applauded her open and candid responses. Her approval ratings went as high as 75 percent evidencing people will endorse those they disagree with, as long as they are listened to with compassion.

With her diagnosis and disclosure of breast cancer and the disfigurement of mastectomy, Betty brought the physical shame and emotional pain, once associated with the topic, out of the shadows. Hundreds of thousands of women across the country scheduled mammograms, saving untold lives. Betty's forthrightness forever changed the perception surrounding the disease.

Even after she left the White House, with no duty or precedent to further disclose her personal life and health challenges, Betty remained a leader. She publicly registered herself into an alcohol and drug rehabilitation program. While others might have avoided the personal disgrace and public mortification of her family's loving intervention, Betty used her position and voice to lead a coalition to help others.

During her personal recovery, Betty discovered that no one was addressing the unique problems rooted in women's addictions. In 1982, with co-founders Leonard Firestone and Dr. James West, she created the non-profit Betty Ford Center in Rancho Mirage, California. For over twenty years Betty's leadership as Chairman of the Board significantly benefited the organization and the population it continues to serve.

IF THERE IS a secret to being an effective communicator, it is first, being a great listener.

During the course of conversation it is common for the person who is waiting to speak, to be caught up in his own thoughts more so than what the other person is saying. In order to drive results, you must hear what others have to say. Leaders listen attentively, also watching body language for clues, so they can respond appropriately to the concerns or questions behind the words.

Pay attention to inferences, as well as the person's remarks, with an open mind. Welcome opposing positions and dissenting opinions. It is *not* important that you concur with or change someone's position. What *is* important is your willingness to be empathic, to listen and learn. Use and welcome constructive feedback.

Practice using simple, concise statements. Clarity is conveyed when every word is relevant. Most importantly, always speak the truth and in doing so, you will earn people's respect and trust. Mike Myatt, leadership advisor to CEOs and contributing author to *Forbes Magazine* said, "People will forgive many things where trust exists, but will rarely forgive anything where trust is absent."

The more engaged and involved a person is, the more effective your message will be. The saying, "People don't care how much you know until they know how much you care" is true. Therefore, replace your ego with empathy. Use communication to clarify the goal and never assume someone understands where you are coming from. Be specific and consistent. In your discussions, relate the message to the larger goals and identify the necessary actions that will need to be taken. Finally, allow the other person to confirm their understanding in their own words.

You will want to measure if your message is meaningful to the other person. A customer's concerns are often different from a co-worker, family member or investor. Ask yourself is your message clear? Have you helped others meet their needs or objectives?

"The art of communication is the language of leadership."

—James Humes,
Author

20
LEADERS ARE ADVOCATES

*"I don't mind being called tough. I am strong.
I do have definite ideas and opinions. In the
sense that 'tough' means that I can take a lot,
stand up to a lot, it's a fair description."*

—*Rosalynn Carter*

ADVOCACY AND LEADERSHIP go hand in hand. It is being of service to others by publicly championing on their behalf and respecting the views and wishes of the person or group they support. An advocate is someone who realizes everyone needs representation, services, opportunities and access to information.

In the political arena, there are literally thousands of advocacy groups (sometimes referred to as lobby groups, campaign groups, or special interest groups) in the United States. They vary in size and influence and use varied methods to campaign for long term social issues, as well as immediate concerns.

Regardless of the issue and irrespective of their size, it takes an influential leader to represent and take on the legislators who have the power to introduce, enact or modify laws. Not all advocacy relates to politics. However, if you want to change regulations, building relationships with and influencing legislators are necessary tools to achieve your goal.

A strong leader and advocate was Rosalynn Carter. Rosalynn's commitment to the mentally disabled began during her husband's (Jimmy Carter) 1970 gubernatorial campaign and continued long after the Carters departed the White House. As a member of the Governor's Commission to Improve Services to the Mentally and Emotionally Handicapped, she was instrumental in the implementation of state-provided services to those in need of aid. Her contribution was invaluable in providing legislative solutions to those dealing with mental illness.

When her husband later ran for the presidency, this dedicated advocate was the first spouse of a candidate to declare her own campaign promise, which was reported this way: "If she became First Lady, she would assume the responsibility for guiding legislative reform on behalf of the nation's mentally ill." This was no small commitment or task, yet one she proudly fulfilled.

As active Honorary Chair of the President's Commission on Mental Health, Rosalynn oversaw 450 volunteers staffing thirty specialized task forces. She also testified on behalf of the Mental Health Systems Act before the Senate Subcommittee on Health.

After leaving the White House, her advocacy continued when she created and chaired The Carter Center's Mental Health Task Force. This advisory body of experts promotes positive changes in the mental health field. Rosalynn Carter's leadership as an advocate lead to legislative reform that protects the lives and rights of any U.S. citizen with a mental illness or disability.

TO ASSIST LEADERS with interest in legislative advocacy, there are a number of schools, centers and national summits that teach the various intricacies involved in advocacy.

The information available is extensive and invaluable in driving change. You can learn: the core fundamentals and skills, advocacy techniques, public relations, strategic planning, organizational development, leading with influence and overcoming resistance.

If political change is your goal, begin at home. It is important you get involved and utilize your good relationship skills. Meet your local district staff members, elected officials and correspond with personalized e-mails. It is vital your correspondence includes: information on the impact a bill would have, reasons for supporting or opposing a bill, and a personal story.

Advocacy is not always about political change. However, regardless of the application, it is a strength worth developing. It is an opportunity to find your voice, face any fears you may have and most importantly, make a difference! Throughout the process, you can educate and inspire others. It builds bonds and friendships with like-minded people and brings about awareness to things about which you feel passionate. Some examples are child abuse, animal rights, maintaining historical buildings, the list is endless.

Whether you advocate for individuals, systems or yourself, you can protect your community, ensure fundamental human needs, provide a positive role model for children today, as well as generations to come. You can change the future.

I could not agree more with dedicated advocacy leader, Dr. Kathryn A. Hughes MD, Fellow of the American College of Surgeons, who passionately wrote: "If you keep quiet because you think your voice does not matter or that you will not be heard, then you will be proven right. If you do not get involved because you think that you will not make a difference, you won't. Only by speaking up can you have the chance to be heard. Only by becoming involved will you have a chance to make a difference. You may be met with indifference or skepticism, even outright opposition. Your audience may be small. The impact of your efforts may seem insignificant. But if you speak, if you act, you can have an effect. Even a small impact matters. It only takes one or two others to hear you speak or to observe your actions to follow your lead and magnify your efforts. The ideas spread; the effect grows. When that happens, you have become a person of influence and a leader."

———∽∾∽———

*"You must be the change you want
to see in the world."*

— Mahatma Gandhi,
Preeminent Leader of India

21

LEADERS ARE
READERS OF PEOPLE

*"There is a saying that a woman is like
a teabag. You don't know her strengths
until she is in hot water."*

—Nancy Reagan

THE ABILITY TO 'read' people has become big business. In a courtroom setting, for instance, a jury consultant is routinely hired for high stake legal cases to ascertain the viability of potential jurors. The consultant must have skilled intuition and keen insight into human behavior and body language. Good leaders recognized this tool long before any name was attached to it. With careful observation, a leader would know if an individual in their organization was in the proper position to maximize his skills or if they were a good fit for the company at all.

Working in the White House and particularly on the president's staff, a strong reader of people is a major asset. Nancy Reagan was the leader who embraced that role and responsibility. Though she was not a staff member *per se,* Nancy was in a unique position. She had an inside view of the White House workings, access to members of the president's cabinet and intimate knowledge of the president's needs. Confident she could somewhat shield her husband from those who wished to exploit the office, Nancy openly stated, "I have strong instincts about people and I'm a good judge of character."

Known for her fierce devotion to her husband, Ronald Reagan, Nancy's primary purpose in life was to help, protect, support, and look after, the one person she called "her hero." Being First Lady gave Nancy an enormous national platform and she gracefully threw herself into the various first lady roles. Any of those duties could have been a full time job, yet she referred to being the president's wife as the "job that outranked them all."

As "Chief Presidential Protector," Nancy was asked if she ever gave her husband advice? "You bet I did. I'm the one who knows him best, and I was the only person in the White House who had absolutely no agenda of her own—except helping him." She went on to say, "I was sleeping with the president, and if that doesn't give you special access, I don't know what does!" Acknowledging President Reagan to be an intelligent, skillful leader in every other sense, "Ronnie can be naive about people around him." Confirming most of her suggestions were about personnel, "Ronnie didn't always take my advice."

Nancy's objections and conflicts with the president's staff were widely publicized. She was furious with the president's

Budget Director David Stockman, whom she read as a "shrewd and crafty man."

Although she felt sorry for Secretary of Labor Raymond Donovan, who was entangled in a fraud investigation, she believed strongly that, "In politics even the appearance of wrongdoing can be enormously damaging." (Although the secretary was eventually acquitted, the ordeal dragged on for months and was "draining both to Ronnie personally and to the office.")

She had a difference of opinion with the Secretary of the Interior and moreover, the president's Chief of Staff Donald Regan. "I told Ronnie repeatedly that he should be fired." Nancy went on to say, "There were also times when I felt that people who had known Ronnie for years were taking advantage of his friendship to pursue their own agendas. Here too, if I thought so, I said so." Nancy was accused and criticized for purportedly having her hand in the firings and/or forced resignations of over twenty people in the Reagan Administration.

Nancy also praised and expressed gratitude for those she felt worked hard for the president and had his best interests at heart. Michael Deaver, Deputy Chief of Staff, was one she worked closely with and considered him a true friend to her husband.

WE KNOW SKILLS can be learned; although it has been said, "...character and attitude, not so much." The subtle intrinsics in an individual's personality are much more defining of their character. Therefore you want to be discerning and look beyond a person's physical appearance, manners and behavior.

Understand that learning how to read people cannot be garnered in some weeklong crash course. Developing the ability takes time and practice. There are a number of different factors involved, such as reading body language, facial expressions and tone of voice. For leadership purposes, I am going to focus on the non-verbal intuitive cues.

Remain objective and insure any information is received neutrally, and without distortion. It is important that a leader be willing to surrender preconceptions and relinquish possible biases on their part. Begin by simply observing. Do not get overly analytical or intense; you are just paying attention and watching. Reserve judgment and take your time.

Do honor your gut feeling and listen to what it is telling you. Gut reactions occur quickly; it's a fundamental response. Particularly during your first encounter, there is an instinctive reaction that occurs, before your brain even has a chance to think. I like to refer to it as my "truth meter." When someone is speaking to you, and you get goosebumps, you are resonating with that person.

Pay full attention during your conversations. Critical insights can be lost as individuals tend to already be thinking of their next thought, even before the person has finished speaking. Something might come to you in a flash and be quickly gone.

Ask pointed questions as opposed to something vague where the person can ramble on. It becomes difficult to detect deception through a person's meandering; also avoid questions easily answered by 'yes' or 'no.'

A good index to a person's character is how he treats people who cannot be of any help to him. True character comes out when no one else can see someone's actions; for instance, does a man keep the ten dollars the person in front of him just dropped when no one is around to see it?

Practice reading people, then get feedback about your accuracy. As your skill improves, you will feel more comfortable adding it to your leadership tool chest.

———⁓———

"The best leaders are readers of people.
They have the intuitive ability to understand
others by discerning how they feel and
recognizing what they sense."
—John C. Maxwell,
Leadership Author

"The power of accurate observation is commonly called cynicism by those who have not got it."

—George Bernard Shaw,
Nobel Prize and Oscar-winning playwright

———❧❧❧———

"Intuition will tell the thinking mind where to look next."

—Jonas Salk,
Medical Researcher

———❧❧❧———

"The best vision is insight."

—Malcolm Forbes,
Publisher of Forbes Magazine

22

LEADERS HAVE A SENSE OF HUMOR

"I married the first man I ever kissed.
When I tell this to my children, they
just about throw up."

—Barbara Bush

HUMOR IS DEFINED in so many ways: anecdotal, black, dark, dry, juvenile, laugh-out-loud, off color, satirical, self-deprecating, slapstick, and witty, just to name a sampling. In fact, humor is a topic of research in the field of psychology. One can actually take a humor personality quiz!

Although types of humor vary from individual to individual, universally it is recognized as one quality the majority of us seek out in others. Numerous surveys indicate that when asked what trait is most sought after in finding a life partner, on average, humor ranks within the top two qualities for women and within the top three for men. (As the participant's ages increase, often times humor is number one.)

Throughout the generations, many of our most admired celebrities are comedians, for example: Robin Williams, Joan Rivers, Jack Benny, Richard Pryor, John Belushi and Sid Caesar. So it is no wonder that leaders embrace humor and utilize it as a strength. According to Dr. Gerald Bell, founder and CEO of Bell Leadership Institute, "Humor is a vital tool of leadership" and "most frequently associated with the best in leaders." Former four-star General and U.S. President, Dwight Eisenhower had this to say, "A sense of humor is part of the art of leadership, of getting along with people, of getting things done."

One such leader, who embraced President Eisenhower's philosophy, was Barbara Bush. She utilized her humor and leadership skills raising six children. Later, on a much larger scale, Barbara made good use of those same skills when she provided service to a nation of children and adults in need of literacy training through the Barbara Bush Foundation for Family Literacy. Only the second woman in history to become both the wife and mother of a U.S. President, Barbara Bush was the country's favorite grandmother for four years.

Laughter and service to others was the foundation Barbara created, while family values remained the corner stone of her life and teachings. Always a fiercely protective "Mama Bear," she was inconsolable when her eldest daughter died of leukemia before her fourth birthday. Like so many other leaders, Barbara choose to turn tragedy into something constructive for others. Throughout her child rearing years and beyond, in addition to her support for leukemia/cancer research, she worked to educate the public regarding the misconceptions of

AIDS, and supported the United Negro College Fund. A strong, competent leader, Barbara defended her traditional views of marriage and motherhood.

By the time her husband, George H. W. Bush then Vice President, ran for the presidency Barbara was a skilled political wife who used her self-deprecating humor in what could have been sensitive situations. From the beginning, to save her husband's staffers any possible embarrassment, Barbara modeled the leadership skills of anticipation, self-confidence and undauntedness when she addressed their concern regarding her grandmotherly appearance. Barbara announced to her husband's campaign staffers, "I love my husband dearly and will do anything to help him...well *almost* anything...I will not lose weight and I will not color my hair!"

Actually, dry humor and quick wit became Barbara Bush's most effective leadership tools. Her ability to tease or joke with reporters was invaluable and often sidestepped the possibility of any controversy. Referring to her move into the White House, Barbara said amusingly, "My mail tells me that a lot of fat, white-haired, wrinkled ladies are tickled pink." At a luncheon, sitting next to the Chancellor of Germany, Helmut Kohl turned to Barbara and said, "It's great to see a lady with a lusty appetite." As opposed to being offend Barbara replied, "Now why doesn't George say something romantic like that?"

During an interview with journalist Jane Pauley, Barbara was asked, "Mrs. Bush, people say your husband is a man of the eighties and you are a woman of the forties. What do you say to that?" Once again she took the high road and responded, "Oh, you mean people think I look forty? NEAT!" She could easily make fun of herself and her wrinkles. Upon seeing two separate pictures, Barbara quipped, "In both (pictures)...it looks as though I had forgotten to iron my face."

The press implied that Barbara, heavy set with white hair, had nothing in common with her petite predecessor Nancy Reagan. Barbara came back with, "Oh but Nancy and I do have a lot in common! We both love our husbands immensely, we both have our causes (Nancy's Just Say No to Drugs, my Fight Against Illiteracy), Nancy wears a size four—my left thigh is a size four."

Then in 1990, when the First Lady was asked to speak at Wellesley College, she received an unexpected and unwelcome reaction from the women students. Many felt she defined herself solely through her husband, with no interests or accomplishments of her own. With a sense of insight Barbara responded, "[I understand] I was twenty myself." In the end, she was well received by all of the students who found her speech to be gracious, serious, and humorous, acknowledging a changing world with women looking to have both a family and career. Ending her talk, Barbara said, "... and perhaps somewhere out there in this audience, may even be someone who will one day follow my footsteps and preside over the White House as the president's spouse...and I wish *him* well!"

HUMOR GOES A long way particularly when people can laugh with you, not at you. It is undeniable that people like to be around those with a pleasant, upbeat personality and will follow those leaders who can get things done and enjoy themselves along the way. Simply put, laughter is healthy and a good ice breaker.

Humor directed at one's self is not only the safest it seems to be appreciated by many. Think of different ways or times in which you could laugh at yourself. Ask your family or close friends to share their amusing memories or humorous stories that involved you. Can you think of times when humor helped you through a tough situation or made a task easier to complete? Everyone has done something silly or embarrassing and it is nice to know that we are not alone.

Years ago I would read "the funnies" from the *Readers Digest*. Each month I would easily find a short (being the optimal word) story, joke or quote, that was appropriate for a particular individual, group, or situation and keep the best ones in a file. The shorter and most relatable ones to you are generally the easiest to remember.

Today with the internet and friends exchanging humorous emails frequently, it is so easy to find a few standard or universal topics that most people will find amusing. Can they be applied to your life in someway? Can you see yourself in a similar situation? Have you made any of the same ditzy comments or drawn pea-brained conclusions? Another good source for humor is today's late night shows, many of which are designed to bring laughter into our daily lives. Listen to how the hosts describe situations or stories. Can some of the timely topics apply to your daily living? Have you run into a similar situation?

I am not suggesting that you need to be a stand-up comic or continual laugh machine. I am saying that leaders look for ways to give their team members a boost. Perhaps there is a subject or issue you need to address with a co-worker, neighbor, or relative that can be discussed in a non-threatening way?

Just as an example, I have a *very* soft spoken friend who had to repeat nearly everything she said to me. I wanted to scream, "For the hundredth time, speak up!" Instead I found a joke about a couple who had a hearing problem. I made the punch line about myself and the difficulty around my elderly hearing, not what I perceived to be her whispering.

You simply want to use humor to be more engaging, help relax those you lead and make the journey more joyful along the way.

———

*"The most wasted of all days
is one without laughter."*

—e. e. cummings,
Poet, Author, and Playwright

23

Leaders Take Calculated Risks

"My feeling is if you're going to be a leader, you have to carefully assess where people are and where people want to go."

—*Hillary Clinton*

I WANT TO be clear: taking calculated risks is not the same as risky behavior. They have two completely different definitions. I am referring to the calculated risks that leaders take to advance their business, sales and even relationships. Leaders understand that taking risks also comes with consequences. Therefore, before leaders do anything, they examine the positive factors against the negative factors, (commonly referred to as the down side) that will always exist.

Without risk takers we would not be where we are today, in every endeavor. In the 21st century, with instant information available around the globe, risk-taking has become a crucial element of leadership. In today's world, innovation moves so quickly, what was effective yesterday may well be obsolete tomorrow. Computers and cell phones are good examples. Mark Zuckerberg, co-founder of Facebook confirmed, "The biggest risk is not taking any risk." Albeit easier said than done, I like to refer to it as, the need to step outside of what feels comfortable, trusting that you are learning and growing.

Just as courage muscles and fearless muscles build with time and experience, so do risk muscles. With preparation, experience and practice, self-confidence continues to broaden and deepen providing the courage necessary to manage fears and confront challenges. These are the two major obstacles that inhibit people from taking risks.

Smart leaders encourage and support their team to think creatively and look for innovative ways of working. Sooner or later, a failure is inevitable. Having a back-up plan is advantageous when possible. Regardless, failure has to be anticipated. More important than failing is what can be learned from it. Learning the 'why' is invaluable, the reasons the plan did not work, what was missing, what opportunity was lost, what question went unanswered.

Thank goodness, the world has risk takers. Today, one of the most widely-known risk takers is Hillary Clinton. Here is a woman who has challenged the glass ceiling for decades.

Many of Hillary Clinton's First Lady predecessors advised their husbands on important political matters. It is commonly known and not unusual for the spouse of a president to act as his personal secretary, review his public speeches, be involved in the hiring of his cabinet members and serve as one of his primary political advisors.

Be that as it may, Hillary was the first to be identified by her husband as a "full partner" and who coined the term "two for one," if he was elected. Within the first week of President Clinton's administration, Hillary stepped into the highly visible role as head of the President's Task Force on Health Care Reform. This was a risky plan that met with considerable stumbling blocks.

Pushing the envelope even further to cement the "two for one" statement, Hillary was the only First Lady to establish an office in the west wing of the White House, where the president's senior staff is positioned.

Some of Hillary's more risky statements, which include, "I guess I could have stayed home and baked cookies" and, her comments on the "vast right-wing conspiracy" (referring to those questioning her husband Bill Clinton's, marital fidelity), failed to convey her objective.

The leader in Hillary persevered. As a sitting First Lady, she sought and won the New York State U.S. Senate seat. When she lost her bid for her party's presidential nomination, Hillary served as Secretary of State, in her adversary's administration.

Hillary Clinton is a trailblazing visionary and confident leader who takes risks and remains determined and focused on her mission to serve; she is again seeking to become the nation's first female president.

TO ENSURE YOU are in fact taking risks and moving outside of your comfort zone, set more challenging goals for yourself. Take on assignments you would normally be fearful of and/

or shy away from. What information do you need to make an educated evaluation of the risk? Make a commitment and accept the challenge of fulfilling or achieving something that has been holding you back.

Write down the opportunities you might pass up or miss if you do not take a particular risk. Weigh those against what you think makes this a risk. Are there individuals who might try to impede your success? If so, how can you avoid their influence? Are there colleagues who can assist or advise you on successfully moving forward? What is the best way to contact those people? Prepare your questions. Be thoughtful of their time.

What is the first, second and third steps you need to take to move forward? Do you have a back-up plan? If you should fail, what did you learn from the process? When you succeed, how will you reward yourself?

It was all-star hockey player Wayne Gretzky who observed, "You miss 100 percent of the shots you never take." The same is true of risks. In the end, it will be the risks you did *not* take, that will cause you regret.

"Progress always involves risk; you can't steal second base and keep your foot on first."

—Frederick Wilco,
Author

24

LEADERS ARE POSITIVE ROLE MODELS

"My husband told me I'd never have to make a political speech. So much for political promises."

— Laura Bush

LEADERS ARE MADE, not born! As demonstrated in previous chapters, I believe anyone can learn leadership skills. It is how you use your leadership abilities that determines if you are a role model for others. Having role models helps us become the person we want to be. Regularly seek out and consider yourself very fortunate if you have a variety of role models (professional, personal, spiritual) throughout your life. When considering a role model, remember it is possible to admire someone's talents, yet choose not to emulate their personal choices.

Role models mean different things to different people. In my view, some of the key attributes are: the ability to overcome obstacles, the acceptance of others, the courage to speak candidly, curiosity, the willingness to learn, being self-challenging and motivating, and leading by example. The greatest role models are an inspiration.

The effect you have on others is greater than you think. Never underestimate the impact of your words, actions and attitude. Rob Liano, author, entrepreneur and sales strategist, cautions, "Each day you are leading by example. Whether you realize it or not, whether its positive or negative, you are influencing everyone around you."

Laura Bush, a former teacher and librarian, understands the power of words, both written and verbal. Armed with a master's degree in library science, Laura lobbied for state funding of early reading and early childhood development programs like, "Ready to Read, Ready to Learn." She also promoted the "Prescription for Reading" program, drawing attention to reading as the key to learning. Thus began the annual and highly successful Texas Book Festival which raises money for the purchase of library books.

She has dedicated her life's work to education across the country and beyond. Believing, "As long as we have books, we are not alone," Laura went on to say, "The power of a book lies in its power to turn a solitary act into a shared vision." A leader who understands the necessity for literacy for all men, women, and children, Laura went to Afghanistan where she promoted a new teacher-training institute for women.

Laura was asked by people who shared her concerns, to represent the United States as honorary Ambassador for the United Nations Literacy Decade. Inaugurating the White House Conference on Global Literacy, she inspired the world leaders in attendance to take this subject to heart.

Authenticity is a rare quality; in politics it is unrivaled in its scarcity. Laura was an exception in the political arena, however. Although she stated publicly, "I would never do anything to undermine my husband's (President George W. Bush) point of view," she felt comfortable speaking candidly when she perceived the president needed some direction. Once on the campaign trail, when she overheard her husband pontificating, she was quoted as saying, "Rein it in, Bubba." On another occasion she joked that, "George and I are complete opposites—I'm quiet, he's talkative, I'm introverted, he's extroverted, I can pronounce *nuclear*."

A true role model for bringing attention to the importance of reading and literacy, Laura Bush is a role model for women in general. Educated, articulate and empathetic, she is consistently praised for her diplomacy.

YOU NEED NOT have a fancy title or possess financial wealth to inspire someone to achieve their greatest potential... to become the best version of themselves. You need only to care and have the desire to be a positive influence, just as role models have influenced you.

For new leaders looking to become role models, this is your practice:

- Know your values and admit your mistakes.
- Demonstrate confidence.
- Show respect and concern for others.
- Express empathy and be humble.
- Give of your time and talent to benefit people outside of your family.
- Be authentic and accountable.
- Model good sportsmanship and be willing to mentor others.
- Share your pathway to success.

For those leaders wondering if they themselves are role models:

- If your influence on someone made them want to be a better person, you are a role model.
- If you have a clear set of values and live those values *everywhere and all the time*, you are a role model.
- If you impressed someone to make the right choice in life, you are a role model.
- If you challenged someone to assist others, you are a role model.
- If you inspired someone to make a difference in the world, you are a role model.

"Example is not the main thing in influencing others. It is the only thing."

—Albert Schweitzer,
Theologian and Nobel Peace Prize recipient

25

LEADERS ARE INNOVATORS

*"We learned about gratitude and humility
— that so many people had a hand in our
success, from the teachers who inspired us to
the janitors who kept our school clean... and we
were taught to value everyone's contribution
and treat everyone with respect."*

—Michelle Obama

WITH EVERY DECADE, we see massive changes in the world. Some of those changes affect the way business is done and some alter the social landscape. The world now operates seemingly at the speed of light, changing business models and objectives. Due to technology and all of its ramifications, from communication to productivity, leadership in the 21st century requires fresh and innovative direction.

Today, high-ranking executives understand that good ideas and creative thinking are not limited to senior staff members. The generations who never used a typewriter or a rotary phone, see and think about the world from a very different perspective.

Since innovation is inherently associated with change, it has become the driving force behind growth and performance. Innovative leaders seek to collaborate with multiple aspects of their organizations. Individuals with differing points of view, contrasting responsibilities, dissimilar backgrounds, experiences and skill-sets can collectively create the type of innovation that one or a few might never uncover.

When talented people are brought together with a clear sense of purpose, there evolves a commitment to embrace the teamwork and its common goal; a synergy occurs that lifts the individual members out of their personal agenda to the group desire for a successful outcome.

The understanding and sole intent of this new corporate model is to cross-fertilize ideas, to initiate, and to inspire creative approaches to a project. Be it ideas for a new concept, improving an original hypothesis and/or finding alternative ways to implement change and solve problems during development, it becomes a shared process.

Innovative leadership is altogether complex; there is no single formula. Innovative leadership involves risk-taking, a willingness to explore ideas, activities and actions with an open mind. When looking for an innovative leader, one needs to look no further than Michelle Obama.

The first African American First Lady, Michelle graduated Princeton University cum laude and Harvard Law School at the age of twenty-four. Her background and education prepared her for today's leadership demands.

Shortly after graduation, Michelle found her true calling in neighborhood community service. Whereas others with her credentials might have sought partnership in a prestigious law firm, she worked in Chicago's City Hall as Assistant Commissioner of Planning and Development. Later, as the founding Executive Director for the Chicago Chapter of Public Allies, her programs helped prepare young people for leadership in public service.

Michelle then brought her innovative leadership skills to the University of Chicago hospitals, initially as Executive Director for Community Affairs, and later, as Executive Vice President for Community and External Affairs.

Demonstrating her support for volunteerism she and Barack Obama, the then president-elect, hosted "a day of service," encouraging millions of visitors to Washington to commit to volunteer service in their local communities.

Today, Michelle continues to advocate for both higher education and healthy living. Michelle supports the Reach Higher Initiative, an innovative approach inspiring young people to take charge of their lives, complete high school and prepare for a career. Her "Let's Move" campaign carries the goal of solving childhood obesity within one generation.

TO HELP YOURSELF mature into an innovative leader, examine where you might improve your current practices while adding these additional skills:

- Perseverance—finding ways to help people obtain solutions.
- Curiosity—making it a core part of your daily living.
- Courage—not fearlessness but more a willingness to act in spite of fear.
- Humility—invite others to challenge your ideas.

When approaching conversations with others, do so with the idea that *they* have ample wisdom in discovering answers. It will assist you in listening for and hearing their astuteness of the topic.

Create a climate of reciprocal trust. Not all innovative ideas are successful, and your team needs to feel safe to stretch their ideas and fail. Generate enthusiasm for innovation by incorporating it in regular business discussions and establishing its importance.

Encourage creativity and ask what changes or improvements your team would like to see in different aspects of your business. Support looking for opportunity in a variety of directions, pursuing boundless possibilities and new ways of thinking. Embrace an innovation mindset, planting seeds of growth and sharing opportunities. In the end, if a project is not working, be willing to scratch it and move on.

"You have all the reason in the world to achieve your grandest dreams. Imagination plus innovation equals realization."

—Denis Waitley,
Author

ABOUT
THE AUTHOR

JACQUELINE BERGER'S CLIMB up the corporate ladder had humble beginnings. As the receptionist at American Savings and Loan (later acquired by Bank of America), it was not long before her talent for working effectively with clients and colleagues drew attention.

Her capacity to calmly manage complex figures and situations fueled her meteoric rise through the ranks, and Jacqueline became the youngest and first female Vice President of Real Estate Lending for a major savings and loan institution. Recognized as an innovator in her field, and then the Western Regional Manager for one of the nations largest Mortgage Insurance Companies, she oversaw all of the high risk lending in six western state offices.

After 25 years in the world of finance lending, Jacqueline ended her corporate career, turning her full attention to a passion that has inspired and informed her life since before her teen years. The day President Kennedy was assassinated began Jacqueline Berger's fascination with America's First Ladies. Encouraged by her closest friends to apply her fervor and distinctive style in telling these women's stories, she 'dove in,' creating what has become a trilogy: *Loves, Lies, and Tears, The Lives of America's First Ladies.* Volumes I and II are currently available. These books and Jacqueline's captivating presentations have earned her a reputation as *"The First Ladies Lady™."*

Jacqueline has discovered an important thread of commonality shared by this unique sorority of women...each was or evolved into a leader whose vision and influence had far-reaching impact. Out of that realization, this book, *Leadership Secrets of America's First Ladies* was born. Between its covers the reader will find practical tools, intriguing questions and plenty of motivation to become a new or better leader.

Ms. Berger, a highly sought after national speaker, resides in Southern California with her husband and family. Her website can be viewed at www.FirstLadiesLady.com.